Segesta 1998

Harold Acton was my Hero

Gay Marks

*t*roubador

Copyright © 1997 by Gay Marks

All rights reserved.
No part of this publication may be reproduced or transmitted in any form or by any means, electronic or mechanical, including photocopy, recording or any information storage and retrieval, without the written permission of the publisher, except for a reviewer who may quote brief passages in review.

Published by
Troubador Publishing Ltd
PO Box 31
Market Harborough
Leics LE16 9RQ, UK
Tel: (+44) 1858 525382
Fax: (+44) 1858 525635
Email: 100113.2636@compuserve.com

ISBN 1 899293 01 9

Harold Acton was my Hero

Gay Marks

To my mother and father

Harold Acton (1904–1994) BA FRSL.
Born: Florence
War service: RAF, Far East
Education: Eton; Christ Church Oxford; Peking University
Honorary titles: CBE 1965, knighthood 1974, *Grande Ufficiale d'Italia*, Knight of the Constantinian Order
Home: *La Pietra*, Florence
Occupation: writer, historian, aesthete
Recreations: 'hunting the Philistines'
Club: the Savile

Gay Marks (1942–   )
Born: London NW6
War service: none
Education: Parliament Hill Grammar School, Guildhall School of Music and Drama, Open University
Honorary titles: none whatsoever
Home: Palermo
Occupation: Teacher of English, struggling writer
Recreations: pondering how life has turned out
Club: Palermo Ladies' Book Club

Note

Although I have changed the names of some of the people in this book out of respect for their privacy, I have kept Charlotte Rampling's in. I do hope she won't mind. I admire her as an actress and secretly, rather covet her sophistication.

I never met Harold Acton during his lifetime or saw a photograph of him. I don't know whether he had a manservant called Giovanni and a cook called Maria, or whether there were basket chairs on the terrace of *La Pietra*, his villa in Florence. Similarly, I have dressed him in clothes of the kind I imagine he might have worn, chosen a wine I think he might have appreciated, and given him friends it is said he entertained. I hope that despite these literary liberties of mine, he would have enjoyed appearing in the pages of this book. I certainly loved having him.

Contents

	Foreword	1
	A Dinner Party	5
1	Waiting Patiently in the Dark	15
2	Much Too Hot	25
3	Bleeding Statues	31
4	Handsome Men, Beautiful Women	45
5	Flora and Fauna	55
6	Temptingly Tranquil	65
7	A Visitors' Guide to Health Matters	73
8	Dust is Feminine	79
9	A Play, a Parcel and Some Sardines	89
10	Palermo	105
11	From Decorators to Manna	113
12	Ms Rampling	123
13	Let There Be Light	127

14	Captain Bland from Yorkshire	133
15	The Strain of Being Chic	139
16	Obbs and Obligations	151
17	Of Nuts, Churches and Markets	159
18	Public and Private	167
19	Solunto	177
	A Phone call	183

Foreword

Let it be inquired whether the first intention of those who are fluttering on the wing, and collecting a flock that they may take their flight, be to attain good, or to avoid evil. If they are dissatisfied with that part of the globe which their birth has allotted them, and resolve not to live without the pleasures of happier climates; if they long for bright suns, and calm skies, and flowery fields, and fragrant gardens, I know not by what eloquence they can be persuaded or what offers they can be hired to stay.

(Samuel Johnson, *A Journey to the Western Islands of Scotland*, 1775)

I live in Sicily, the large triangular island set right in the heart of the Mediterranean. Although everyone has heard of the Mafia and Mount Etna, they may well be a little vague about the rest. Sicily has an ideal climate, celestial food, a subtropical brilliantly-coloured flora and crystal seas – the sort of place one should be able to be eternally happy in.

An old joke says that when God finished fashioning Sicily and realised that he had created Eden, he hurriedly decided to redress the balance in case the other inhabitants of the Earth should be envious, and so he put the Sicilians there. The joke which the islanders tell against themselves, is supposed to justify what a lot of British holiday-makers out here see as a charming, happy-go-lucky attitude to life. For some of us living permanently on the island, it's not always such rollicking fun.

The other day for instance, I had my wallet stolen on a crowded lunchtime bus. Usually fanatically careful about my personal belongings – keeping them in a buttoned pocket rather than in my easy-to-open handbag – I had momentarily removed my protective hand. The wallet was gone in a moment. I went to report the theft at the *carabinieri* station.

"Pickpocket, bag snatching, mugging or burglary?" I was asked

"Pickpocket."

"This way please."

I was shown into a tiny room containing an oversized *carabiniere* in his black and red uniform behind an antiquated typewriter, and asked to sit down. A wad of papers interleaved with carbon was rolled laboriously into the machine:

"Name?"

Carabinieri are generally kind-hearted and uncomplicated people. A feeble but evergreen joke says they always go around in pairs as one of them does the reading, the other the writing. Certainly they tend to be from the *paesi* or country towns and villages, and invariably are men of great girth and swarthiness.

After ten minutes I was handed my written statement to sign. It was covered with black thumb marks.

"Why is there a question mark after my name ?" I wanted to know.

He took the paper back. "That's the typewriter: when you press comma, it prints question mark."

My address had been spelt wrong and I was Manks instead of Marks but I let it go; after all I was never going to see the money again.

I can never make up my mind whether things should change out here; whether for instance developing its coastline and mountain villages for large-scale tourism would spell life or death to the island; there's a definite charm in its crumbling urban decay and miles of wild deserted beaches. At the same time, Sicily desperately needs a massive economic boost.

It's a terrible dilemma.

But then I'm English – and illogically so. I want the best of both worlds. Oddly enough, most of us seem to get on surprisingly well out here. Maybe it's because we're an insular people like the Sicilians themselves; maybe it's because like them, we feel ourselves to be in some way "different". But different from what and whom: the continent, America, Africa? That wouldn't surprise me at all. What we mean is that we English are individualistic and totally unlike other Europeans, and we tend I think, to be proud of this diversity. I have clung to my Englishness because such tenacity has been inculcated into me. I could quite as easily slip into being a Sicilian if I wanted to. It is just that I won't let myself.

This inner tug-of-war reminds me a bit of E. M. Forster's *Passage to India* in which nice Mr Fielding who teaches in the local English college, is begged by his Indian friend Aziz to "give into the East" and stay in India with him.

That "giving in" has haunted me for years: the relinquishing of home ties, the relaxing of out-of date principles, the acceptance of other ways of looking out at the world. The enormous relief of *letting go*. Fielding wasn't able to and nor am I. I may be physically present on Sicilian soil, but I'm still terribly English.

In spite of that, I am still here – in, I suppose, one of Doctor Johnson's happier climates. The burden of my own insularity sits slightly less firmly on my shoulders nowadays I must admit – in fact it's definitely slipping. But – a bit to my own surprise – it is still there.

4   Harold Acton was My Hero

A dinner party

Before this book went to press I decided to give a dinner party. It was mainly for Harold Acton who had inspired the whole thing in the first place. Apart from his fame as an aesthete, not a great deal is known I would imagine about this most famous of expatriates and lifelong resident of Italy. What fascinated me about him was the status he so obviously enjoyed in Tuscany, and the elegance of the wide circle of literati he entertained over the years in his Florentine villa – writers like Evelyn Waugh and Somerset Maugham as well as such fine examples of Anglo-Saxon drollery as the Sitwells.

His civilised and cultured Anglo-Italian world contrasted so very violently with my own in Palermo, that I thought I'd take a look at what in fact makes for the successful expatriate and how such a status can be reached and maintained. Is it for instance the ability to hang onto one's Englishness in the face of all odds, or the skill perhaps in shielding visiting countrymen from the chaos of southern Italian life? I'm quite sure Harold never had to defend his place in the supermarket queue, suffer a water shortage or give his opinions on the Mafia.

The second guest at my dinner party was Dr. Johnson whom I've quoted at the beginning of the book and who was so often in my thoughts as I wrote. Johnson had never managed to get to Italy and I very much wanted to ask him whether he felt he'd missed out on something. I wanted to see too how he and Harold got on together.

I had also invited James Joyce who did in fact make it to Italy – and who like me had lived there and taught in the Berlitz School of Languages. Although I can't admit to liking Joyce, I had this compulsive desire to hear what he had to say about Trieste where he had taught and what he thought of the people there. I had an instinctive feeling I would be the more credible of the two when it came to analysing the Italian psyche. As the day got nearer, I wondered if I'd made a ghastly mistake in asking Joyce but the invitations had gone out and it was too late to do anything about it. I only hoped he wouldn't ruin the whole evening for everyone.

My fourth and final guest was the Queen; my reason for inviting her was that she had been to Palermo in 1980 when I was still working at the British Consulate. I had been one of the first people she had met as she came into the great hall where the British community had been assembled. I wanted to know what had struck her most about Palermo.

I asked my husband Franco if he wanted to be present as well but he said definitely not, that they were my guests and that I could get on with it.

I agonised over the menu for about a week before deciding on a fairly safe pasta dish to start with: ribbed *pennette* with fried aubergines and tomato. It was touch and go between that and the typically Sicilian *pasta coi broccoli arriminati* made with cauliflower florets, onion, pine nuts and garlic, all simmered together and then spread thickly over a steaming mound of spaghetti. Cauliflower as everyone knows, makes an unbearable smell when it's cooking and English people never feel socially at ease dealing with long strands of pasta, so I abandoned that idea. Besides, even if I had used short, chunky shapes, I didn't think my guests – especially Harold and the Queen – would appreciate such a robustly southern dish.

For the same reason I played safe and decided on grilled swordfish steaks with capers for the main course, served with one of my special mixed salads. Swordfish is just foreign enough to be interesting but not so exotic as to upset people by coming to the table with its eyes and fins still on. It does not have any nasty little bones either. Dessert was to be coffee ice cream cake bought from the confectioner's behind the gasworks.

The seating arrangements gave me a bit of trouble; we were to eat in the kitchen at the round table. It's a lovely large room with a view over the Favorita park to the mountains beyond, and I planned to put the Queen with her back to the fridge so she could look out. On her left I put Harold and on her right Dr. Johnson. Joyce came between Harold and myself so that I then had the doctor on my left. My only worry was that I might have to ask the Queen to shift her chair if I needed to get more wine from the fridge.

Drink of course was another problem. The coarse white wine from Alcamo we usually drink packs a tremendous punch and really didn't seem right for the occasion – not that I thought Joyce would have found any fault with it. Instead, I plumped for two bottles of the cool sophisticated Sicilian Regaleale and, in honour of Harold, two of the full-bodied red Brunello di Montalcino Riserva from Tuscany.

There also had to be ale for Johnson, as well as an after-dinner liqueur for everyone. This I chose without any qualms: the celestial Caffé Sport whose rich sweet vapours rise up into the nostrils, winding their way into the internal cavities and bringing tears of sweet anticipation to the eyes.

Harold Acton and Dr. Johnson were the first to arrive, sharing the lift up to my fourth-floor flat.

"Gay Marks!" Harold kissed my hand. "At last!"

He was wearing beige slacks, a pale pink open-necked shirt with a paisley cravat and soft leather mocassins. He looked cool and relaxed.

Behind him, panting a bit, came Johnson in a heavy dun-coloured flared coat reaching to his knees and with turned-back cuffs, grey breeches, white stockings and black buckled shoes. His wig, I couldn't help noticing, sat a bit crookedly on his head. He made a deep bow.

"Madam, I am honoured to make your acquaintance."

"Do come in both of you" I said, and held out my hand for Johnson's three-cornered hat, "I thought we'd sit out on the balcony as it's so warm."

Although this was mid-October, it really was very warm. I was pleased that everything looked so lovely outside, with the lights of Palermo twinkling in the distance and my climbing jasmine in full flower already scenting the evening air.

Just as I got them settled in the white plastic garden chairs on the balcony, the downstairs buzzer went again. This time it was James Joyce, scarlet in the face and tapping a rolled-up copy of the *Corriere della Sera* dangerously against his thigh.

"Good evening to you" he managed to get out between his teeth, "at LAST."

"Mr. Joyce" I said scenting trouble "I am *so pleased* you were able to come. I expect you're ready for a drink after your long journey."

"Bloddy hot weather you have in this island." He had caught sight of the

Glen Grant on the table and was softening up. I thought what an unattractive specimen he was, thin-lipped, bespectacled and with belligerent, flaring nostrils.

"Who's that you've got out there?" he said jerking his head towards the two figures on the balcony as I put a glassful of whisky into his hand.

"That's Dr. Samuel Johnson and Sir Harold Acton" I said soothingly, and I'm expecting the Queen any minute now."

This news had an immediate effect on my three guests; Harold's head snapped towards me.

"The Queen? You didn't say anything about that on the invitation."

"I thought you'd be pleased," I said, "all of you."

"My dear lady" began Johnson starting to heave himself out of his plastic chair, "I'm afraid you have acted incorrectly. If one is expected to share a dinner table with the monarch, one comes adequately attired and prepared."

"But you are, Dr. Johnson" I began "and she does so want to meet you. I'm sure nobody needs to stand on ceremony at all."

He was breathing heavily. "Do let me give you a glass of...of ale" I finished weakly.

"If the English Queen wishes to come to your home, that is up to her" Joyce said taking a pull of his whisky and stepping out onto the balcony. He nodded to Harold and Dr. Johnson. "I myself have no particular wish to meet *her*, of that I can assure you all."

"Well well" Harold was musing to himself, "I haven't seen Liz since last Spring. What on earth is she doing in Sicily?"

"She's very kindly come down to attend this dinner" I said rather piqued by the way he said "Sicily". And then: "what can I get you to drink, Harold? I do hope I can call you Harold?"

"Of course you may my dear. Well, I'd rather like a gin if you have one. Lemon and a dash of water."

The buzzer went for the third time. I picked up the entry phone.

"It's Queen Elizabeth" came the disembodied voice, "what floor?"

"Oh good evening Your Majesty" I said, "fourth."

I heard the lift click into action.

"What does the Queen drink?" I asked Harold. I hadn't thought of that.

"She doesn't actually" he said, "just half a glass of wine sometimes to be convivial."

We were all standing when the Queen entered. Dr. Johnson I noticed was extremely ill at ease, twitching his face muscles and straightening the lapels of his thick coat. Harold opened both arms wide:

"Elizabeth!" (not Liz I noted) "how lovely to see you!"

I shook her hand. "May I introduce Dr. Samuel Johnson and Mr. James Joyce?"

Johnson kissed her hand making rather a botched job of it, Joyce managed his handshake somewhat better.

"It is a great pleasure to meet you Ma'am."

"And for me."

She looked at Sam. "And how very glad I am to meet you too at last Dr. Johnson. I have heard so much about you. What a delightful room and how kind of you to ask me Mrs. Marks.* You must be very happy living in such a beautiful country." She let Harold take her cardigan. "How are you, dear Harold? I had no idea you were going to be here. What a treat this is for me!"

She looked pleasing and attractive in a loosely-fitting powder blue silk dress patterned all over with tiny white mushrooms, and wore no hat.

* * *

Before anyone was able to get to grips with the first forkful of pasta, Harold Acton cleared his throat and stood up.

"Er... may I just say Gay how flattered and honoured I am that you are to name your book after me" (Well, not exactly, I thought).

"I cannot see how I could possibly be *anybody's* hero!" His low-pitched laugh set his thorax pulsating and made his shoulders heave rhymically up and down six or seven times." I was enchanted" he went on "by your book." (I had sent a synopsis and a few specimen pages to all my guests with their invitations), "and am looking eagerly forward to reading the rest of it."

"Hear hear!" This from the Queen.

"Let me very briefly go on to say (as I am now on my feet!) that I am, like you, one of the English in exile. But *voluntary* exile. Italy – and Florence in particular – has been my home for as long as I can remember

---

*Although the Queen refers to me as Mrs. Marks, this is not my married name. Marks is my maiden name and the one I write under. In Italy a woman keeps her maiden name even after marriage.

and I can truthfully say there exists no lovelier place on Earth..."

I heard a muffled splutter from Johnson.

"Unhappily, I am not as familiar with Sicily as I should like to be, but am told that it too is of great beauty and interest, and I look forward to discovering some of it in the short time I have left at my disposal here. Although I must admit to finding it somewhat...more, how shall I say?....*exuberant* than expected. Huh-huh-huh-huh-huh-huh-huh- huh. But this isn't surprising; at my age one feels happier among the familiar objects of one's home and garden – one's cat and manservant – the life one has built up over the years, and that is how it should be. You have had a quite different experience to mine and I am confident no less varied for that. I wish you every success with your book."

He sat down.

"Thank you so much" I said and leant across the table to put my hand over his.

I couldn't help feeling we had made a dreadful faux pas in not letting the Queen speak first, but it must be all right if Harold had begun the proceedings; he should know the form after all. And so it turned out. I looked across

at her and saw she was now gathering herself together as if to rise.

"I'm not much of a public speaker as my friends know (thank you Harold for starting the ball rolling). People of course always assume that I must be, which makes it quite awkward for me. Thank you Mrs. Marks for giving me the chance of visiting Sicily again. I found it a fascinating place the first time I came.

You know, I have had several books by British people living abroad given to me over the years – the last one written by some woman with a foreign double-barrelled name, which I'm afraid I just couldn't get into. Then there was the other one about France... Peter something or other. That I'm afraid to say ended up in the WPB after the first few pages. One must be *really* and *truly* part of the world one is writing about to understand it, don't you agree? The amused observer just won't do. I also believe most firmly that each of us has a duty to get to know our fellow human beings. And to tell those of us who stay at home about them.

I could go on quite a bit about what happened on that last visit to Sicily (you see Harold, I've lost my nervousness now!) but this is your evening my dear Gay Marks. Just to say that the Mediterranean has always held a particular magic for me and I believe for all those who come here. I'm sure you have done it justice. My very best wishes to you."

Dr. Johnson made an odd growling noise as though he had an apple core stuck at the back of his throat and then he too pushed back his chair and slowly stood up. He bowed solemnly to the Queen and then turned to me.

"It would be untruthful of me Madam" he began dropping his eyes almost immediately, "to give an honest judgement of your work when I have not yet had the pleasure of perusing it to its full extent. However, I am of the opinion that any English man or woman able to live in a foreign country for as many years as you yourself have done – and especially in those Mediterranean lands which differ so markedly from our own culture – merits the highest praise."

I saw Acton smile.

"As you are no doubt aware, this is the first time I have set foot on Italian soil, having travelled from London directly to the Isle of Sicily only yesterday, and I am struck most forcibly by the singular behaviour of its inhabitants and by its temperamental climate...."

I was beginning to get worried about the pasta growing cool on our plates, but he was in full swing.

"One may observe the human race in all its forms and manifestations with the greatest of interest, thus gaining knowledge and wisdom with which to enrich ourselves; I myself have visited the shores of France and the Isles of Scotland and have been not unfavourably impressed by much of what I have seen. However, I feel obliged to own to this company that my heart and soul reside – and will do so forever – in our own beloved England which you Ma'am" (and here he raised his eyes and inclined his head respectfully towards the Queen) "preside over with such grace and dignity."

At this point Joyce's voice could be heard in a petulant little-boy undertone: "I do indeed come from Ireland but I cannot help it. Boo-hoo!"

Johnson pretended not to hear. "My dear Gay Marks" he said now turning towards me full face so that I saw for the first time his thick pitted skin and full mobile lips "let me congratulate you on your steadfastness in resisting for so long among foreigners, for they are uncommonly unlike ourselves." (He didn't know, or had forgotten, that I had married a Sicilian.) "This is a very personal choice which I am bound to respect even though I cannot share it. I very much hope however that in describing the Sicilians in the pages of your book, you have exercised fairness, tolerance, compassion and humility, for these are the qualities that ennoble us in God's eyes."

He sat down quite suddenly and there was a short surprised silence. Then Joyce got to his feet.

"Your Majesty and people of England. I am an Irishman and proud of it" (you old liar I thought, you couldn't stand the place). "That notwithstanding, I have lived most of my life abroad. Trieste, where I exercised my teaching abilities, was my first port of call and it was there that I first learned the rudiments of the Italian language." He opened his arms dramatically and addressed the kitchen ceiling: "

"Avevi la più bella fica che avessi mai visto O divina, ed io imploravo una tua carezza!"

This was most dreadfully obscene and I glanced in horror at the Queen but she was smiling blandly.

"Many good friends did I make in that lovely city" Joyce went on "and many were the fine drinking nights we spent together. Gay Marks!" he shot out at me so suddenly that I jumped, "Gay Marks! If you have read my finest literary achievement which goes by the name of *Ulysses*....you have read it so, have you not?"

"Well, I did try, really, but I'm afraid I couldn't get...."

"That's no matter. I haven't read yours either and have no intention of doing so. Well, but in those fine pages of mine I make reference to the noble land of Italy, land of golden wine and sun...."

Dr. Johnson was showing signs of impatience, jabbing irritably at a piece of aubergine in his pasta.

"... and I have no earthly reason for criticising this island which on the contrary I notice is full of jollity, light and happy faces and....." he raised his glass "of fine whisky. So I shall praise it. Gay Marks, I am sure you have done a fine job. May your book sell millions of copies and may the Sicilian race go from strength to strength! Let the feast begin!"

The swordfish I would say was probably the most successful part of the meal. That and the crusty Palermo bread which greatly interested Johnson.

"Exceedingly fine, Madam" he said crumbling it in his fingers and holding it under his nose "and with an uncommonly good taste. We have nothing to rival this in London at all."

That pleased me a great deal.

We also got through four bottles of Alcamo white wine without even touching the posh Tuscan Brunello. By the time we got to the port and liqueur, Joyce was illustrating the steps of an Irish jig to the Queen, singing hoarsely as he did so:

> Ah, Tim Finnegan lived in Walkin Street
> A gentleman Irish mighty odd...

Harold Acton, legs elegantly crossed, was having an argument with Johnson over the merits of expatriation.

"There are a great many reasons for choosing to live abroad you know," he said with a smile.

"Sir, a man who loves his country will not willingly abandon it, and there's an end to the matter" said the doctor. His wig had slipped right down over his forehead and he was sweating profusely.

"Do please take your coat off if you feel too hot, Dr. Johnson" I said to him.

"Not in the presence of ladies, for that would be discourteous. But I thank you for your concern."

> Now Tim had a sort of a tipplin' way
> With the love of the liquor he was born...

As the jig came to an end, the Queen collapsed laughing onto her chair and looked at her watch, "Twenty to one! My goodness I must be going. Can I give anybody a lift?"

Harold and Dr. Johnson left with her in the Rolls. Joyce had fallen into a stupor out on the balcony and I decided to leave him there. I could see to him tomorrow.

1
Waiting patiently in the dark

What am I doing on this island anyway? I am not a citizen of the world, let alone Europe, and never will be. What am I doing attending jumble sales in the Anglican church? I don't want a St. Peter's Square snowstorm paper weight or a smelly Forties' edition of Pearl S. Buck; and I defy anyone born in West Hampstead N.W.6 to get excited over how many boiled sweets there are in the jar. Yet this is what I find myself doing.

Why I wonder do I feign interest in the English film club (*Tootsie, Fatal Attraction*) and the visits of H.M. Royal Navy to Palermo? Do I really, really care about the arrival of the new English Chaplain and his lady wife in the city?

As may be obvious, none of these curious goings-on have the slightest relevance to English life as it is today. It's more a prop for the homesick, for the clinging-on members of a long-forgotten and never to be regained England. Here though, we're not in New Zealand (which someone once told me is thirty comfortable years behind the Mother country) or in Maugham's tropics in the thirties; this is Europe today. This is Palermo, Sicily, just two hours and forty minutes flying time from Luton airport.

Just why such an extraordinary state of affairs has lasted well into the nineties must have something to do with that tenacious and rather unhealthy attachment to national identity some of us still seem to have. No English person in their right mind you will say could be so morbidly attached to

Marmite, or red jelly or Christmas crackers. Some really are.

But to get back to what I am doing here apart from chronicling this strange world. I arrived in Palermo in October 1963 to fill in a gap before what I supposed was going to be work in London. This Sicilian year was to be fun and warm. Like addled old James Joyce who went to Trieste, I had been hired to teach in the Berlitz School of Languages, and (maybe again like him) I hadn't a single word of Italian.

"Much better, much better" the director insisted when I told him of this lacuna, "they learn more quick."

"They" in fact by some miracle did manage to learn something but whether more quick or not I don't know. I hadn't the slightest idea about grammar – neither how to break it down nor how to teach it. I couldn't even have told you how many tenses there were (are?) in the English language. At least my spelling was good, which it certainly isn't now.

I rented an attic in what is known in Italian as a *quartiere popolare*, a joyfully dirty working class area. The flat was only one room with a large stone sink on the roof outside into which I used to clamber bodily to wash. I paid the equivalent of £6 a month for it, I remember. It's a bijou residence now with variegated geraniums spilling down over the terrace wall.

There were very few English in Palermo then, only a handful of Americans and Irish, and that was it. Most of us taught. The Sicilians were totally mystified at why we had come in the first place and appalled at our intention to stay.

"You can't possibly like it here" they said again and again, "it's uncivilised."

You don't hear quite so much of that today, which is slightly unnerving – especially as I had grown used to being thought civilised. Unfortunately for our English self-esteem, a general levelling-out of social and moral values has brought both islands much closer together. No longer are we the envied perpetrators of "the queue", of self-control (with the accent on the first o), and quiet unhurried elegance. And it serves us right; complacency is a dangerous state.

British phlegm however hasn't completely lost its newsworthiness, and still earns an occasional snigger in the Italian press. The report of a recent tube breakdown for instance spoke of hundreds of Londoners waiting in orderly silence and total darkness for the electricity to be restored.

Quite *incredible*.

"What would Sicilians have done?" I asked knowing exactly what the answer would be.
"Panicked and screamed" came the prompt reply.
"Really? Why?"
"Because that's the way we are."
If Sicilians can't keep their cool, we English are strangely unpredictable: football riotors, "ooligans" and heavy drinkers for instance. But these, as I always point out, are not exactly English, but *British* maladies. The Sicilians, who do not wreck their stadiums or have pubs in which to drink themselves silly, seem confused by this.
"English means from England and British means from Wales or Scotland basically" I used to tell my students.
"Ah."
"I mean, if you're Welsh, you call yourself British, not English."
"Not Welsh?"
"Or Welsh, yes."
"But you who are from London, Gay, would not call yourself British?"
"Well no; no I wouldn't. I'm English."
"Mm."
Just as we claim not to understand why Latin people panic on the tube train instead of waiting patiently in the dark, they find our excessive alcohol consumption puzzling. The difference between us is that we criticise, and they don't.
"The further south you go in Europe", I once heard a father telling his young son at Gatwick airport, "the less you find people are able to organise themselves". While this may very well be true, I nevertheless felt it a crude judgement to make; it also upset me rather as I live about as far south as you can go in Europe. People I reminded myself – and especially children – should make up their own minds about what disorganisation implies and whether in fact it can be counted as a positive quality or a shortcoming.

* * *

The language school where I worked had an odd crop of teachers – all of whom I soon discovered knew as little as I did about didactic methods and grammar rules. We were meant to follow the Berlitz method with our adult learners, using a much-fingered and stained hardback which began

This is a pencil.

If all went well, students then progressed to

this is a pen

and, containing their mounting excitement, to

it is not a pencil.

The hours were odd: 4–9pm non-stop, and the pay, although not over-generous, nevertheless allowed us to live quite comfortably. Not many of our students were overkeen to learn English; most of the young women were probably filling in time before marriage or doing something they could talk to their friends about, and the men were only slightly more motivated. Behaviour however was very correct and very few of the men ever tried anything on – they'd probably been severely warned beforehand by the director. Foreign girls teaching in Sicilian language schools was still a relatively innovative event in the sixties, and the school had a name to protect.

After a while we started siphoning off students, persuading them to come to us privately so we could make more money. I had moved from the attic by that time and was sharing a flat with two Dublin girls in a more upmarket area of town.

One unattractive middle-aged student we approached had been pleased and flattered to leave the classroom and come to us privately. Tuesday morning was his day and he was my pupil. His name was Alfredo and he looked like the mass murderer Christie from Rillington Place – fawn raincoat and all.

"A-L-F-R-E-D-O" he would mouth at me coming up very close to my face, "that's an easy name to pronounce: Al-*fray*-doh". He had terrible breath.

He always arrived bang on time with a flat briefcase under his arm. As I never remembered he was coming and was still in bed on Tuesday mornings, this meant he had to wait for me in the sitting room on one of the hard-backed wooden chairs, shod feet neatly together on the thinning carpet.

One morning, the cat who lived with us leapt up into my lap during the English lesson. Alfredo leant forward to stroke the cat and in doing so made sure he stroked my breasts too. I can still see his nostrils flaring with lust. That was the last time he came.

Another student was the poor runtish Maurizio who again carried a flat briefcase and who walked everywhere very swiftly, leaning into the wind. He was not quite right in the head and wore very thick glasses. His overriding passion was the tenor Beniamino Gigli, and he owned nearly all his original recordings. During the lessons at the school he would explain the finer points of Gigli's technique, breaking off to sing bars very loudly and with great feeling, swaying backwards and forwards in his seat. It got quite embarrassing. Until quite recently I still used to catch glimpses of him, one shoulder held slightly higher than the other, as he hurried along under the plane trees in Via Libertà.

As well as his attachment to Gigli, we sensed Maurizio harboured an unhealthy interest in foreign girls, and after the cat incident, decided not to secure him as a private student.

I had some ridiculous ideas about life on the Continent then. One was that I should do all my shopping from street stalls like I'd seen people doing in Italian films – the more haggling the better, and that to go to supermarkets was somehow cheating. There weren't many supermarkets about in those days anyway, just dark, evil-smelling groceries with flies crawling painfully slowly over gently sweating cheeses. Nevertheless, I'd made up my mind that I'd stride through the city's markets like Sofia Loren, shoulders well back, bosom and chin proudly uplifted, swinging an open-work basket as I went and putting down the lewd calls of the stall-holders with withering, disdainful glances.

Things didn't go that way at all. To start with I couldn't make myself understood. Greengrocers would stare at me uncomprehendingly pointing first at aubergines then at broccoli while I shook my head. I couldn't even get out the phrase "two rolls please" at the bakery, or count my change properly. I didn't look the part either.

Years later and having given up the idea of being Sofia Loren, I've come to realise that although shopping may be a very ordinary activity, it still demands a great deal of give and take in Italy; you could say it's a question of every woman for herself with the weakest going irretrievably under.

The good Sicilian housewife, for instance, always shops with a frown; this is to show she means business and doesn't intend to be fobbed off with mouldy old tomatoes or gristly meat. In fact if you take a look at shoppers anywhere in Palermo you'll see a bevy of furious-looking women prodding, pinching and smelling the wares. Not a smiler among them. At the butcher's for instance, the woman in front of me eyes the skinned rabbits with deep suspicion. In the end she decides on steak.

"Now it must be tender – *very* tender" she insists, "no fat whatsoever. None at all. My husband's got no teeth you know and just can't manage any tough meat." She turns round to the customers behind her "No teeth" she reiterates," can only eat the very finest, most tender cuts."

The butcher takes this information in silence. Although he has never seen the woman before, the news of her husband's dental problems are accepted as part of the normal selling process.

Another woman attempts to push in front of me. I remind her firmly that she arrived after I did.

"I know, I know, but I've got my sick old mother at home" she tells me "I'm in a terrible hurry."

Sick old mothers and toothless husbands are run of the mill characters in Palermo, and ones I have got perfectly used to dealing with over the years. It doesn't do to consider them with too much compassion if you value your time.

Bread is bought without undue incident, still warm from the oven and served by a girl with beautiful dark eyes. Every loaf piled up behind her in the wooden compartments has a different name which as a customer I am expected to know. "One of those, please" just won't do; there's the name for the very long, the quite long, the plaited, the worm-cast, the round, the with-salt and the without-salt, the white and the wholemeal, the olive and the tomato bread. Then there are all the rolls and the breadsticks: with or without a covering of seeds, the biscuits, brioches and pizzas – all sizes and shapes and all named. After years of speaking the language I still don't know them all.

It is extremely hot in the baker's and most people are shouting – again quite a normal state of affairs. Raised voices do not necessarily indicate wrath, they are more a way of making one's presence known. Money changes hands at a furious rate at the till with coins being slapped down noisily on the counter. Italian fiscal law stipulates that all retailers have to issue a receipt for every article sold and that includes one bread roll. So together with your wares you have to wait for a long worm of printed paper to come snorting out of the cash register. Failure to collect your receipt

makes both you and the shopkeeper liable to a heavy fine.

I decide to pick up a bus on the way back as the shopping is heavy. Tickets which are purchased at tobacconists have to be automatically stamped on the bus itself. Again, failure to comply leaves you open to another heavy fine, although I have never seen or heard of the law being applied. Invariably (especially if you are a woman) the inspector will direct you quite kindly towards the machine or else ask other passengers if they have a spare ticket to sell.

This morning the bus comes to a sudden halt in the middle of the road as the driver recognises a friend driving the other way. Leaning out of their respective windows, both men start a lengthy chat, nodding and gesticulating animatedly while the traffic piles up behind in both lanes. Again, nobody on board seems unduly put-out by the delay, and even begins to take quite an interest in the conversation.

There would be nothing particularly surprising about any of this until one realises that Palermo is not in fact a backward third-world village but part of Italy – the same Italy which contains such dauntingly efficient and economically successful northern enclaves as Bologna and the tidy well-run jewels of Ravenna or Pavia. What's more, it is a large bustling city of one million inhabitants.

* * *

In the old days I preferred to walk the mile or so from my tiny attic flat in the *quartiere popolare* to the Berlitz rather than take the bus, but this was only because I had no idea how to answer the bus conductor if he were to speak to me.

One day it must have been raining pretty hard because I remember standing at the bus stop with several other people. We seemed to have been there for an unusual length of time when a battered, dark-blue minibus drew up and stopped. There was an immediate scuffle round me as people fought to bundle in.

"Are you coming in or not, Signorina?" the driver called to me. How kind I thought, there must be another bus strike, and I clambered in. The van was packed with dour-faced men and women clutching shopping bags and steaming in their plastic macs and rainhats; it smelt of wet wool and stale cigarette smoke.

I had got the last bit of available seat. Nobody spoke as we bowled along filthy old Corso Olivuzza with its rushing gutters and piles of rubbish, and turned left towards the Politeama Square in the heart of the city. I saw sodden people at bus stops angrily waving their arms as we drove past, but the driver only grunted and kept going.

At the next stop someone slid back the sides of the van and most of us got out. I thanked the driver and began walking away thinking how lucky I'd been.

"Hey! Hey, you! Where d'you think you're off to?"

"What?" I said turning round

"That's a hundred and fifty lire." He was aghast at my affrontery.

My faith in human kindness had been totally misplaced. It had never occurred to me that I had to pay.

* * *

There is a register office in Palermo for the issue of various certificates: certificates of residence, marriage and so on. So chaotic was it at one time and so overcrowded that it became notorious even among the city's inhabitants. I remember going there once and having to fight through its jam-packed hall; queueing was physically impossible. Shoes, buttons and bags were ripped off or dropped and lost for ever; shouting men and sobbing old women surged forward in an attempt to reach the correct window to collect their documents. Nothing I have experienced before or since has been able to compare with it.

Part of the problem of course is the Italian mania for certificates. Apart from the perfectly normal pieces of paper required for chronicling rites of passage, an Italian applying for a job must also present written proof that he has never been in prison. Another document known as *esistenza in vita* literally "alive", has just that function: to prove you haven't died in the previous fiscal year. This of course is vitally important it you wish to go on receiving your pension.

There is no point here in listing the numerous other bits of paper you need to get by; far from being delightful little nuggets of folklore, they are tragic realities – both for us who have to pay for them and because they suck away public money by providing totally unnecessary jobs for civil servants.

So far, nothing comparable to Italian red tape exists in England; all the same, we've got plenty of nasty stuff ourselves that nobody else wants. I got a very uncomfortable feeling seeing Ken Loach's film *Raining Stones*. It was showing at a local cinema club that screens non-commercial films – the sort that have picked up special awards or prizes at Cannes and Venice; low-budget films from Britain or Eastern Europe that use unknown actors or non-actors and are full of four-letter words and vomiting.

Raining Stones, set in Greater Manchester, is a story of poverty, violence, unemployment and degradation and is one of the most depressing and demoralising films I've seen. Comments on this ghastly waste of money, overheard afterwards in the foyer and later read in the press, were uncannily similar. Both in fact showed fear of Italy going the same way.

Few things I think can be more soul-destroying than an English council estate in the rain. No matter how foul and disgusting Palermo or Neapolitan slums are, they are nevertheless made bearable by the lovely warm sunshine, and most foreigners seem to agree that the washing slung across their alleyways is picturesque rather than squalid. But the sun doesn't shine that much in Greater Manchester, the concrete tenements are grey and peeling, the windows mean. This is the face of Britain I definitely do not wish to be reminded of; it makes me shiver with horror.

2
Much too hot

It was getting too hot to work, to think or even to rest and I got up to lower the slatted sun blinds and switch on the ceiling fan. Houses in Sicily are built – or should be built – to minimise the heat, and most of those that went up before the sixties were. They had high ceilings, thick walls and narrow, heavily shuttered windows. The further back you go in fact, the cooler the buildings. The Arab mosques, Norman castles and churches are the best places of all to be in summer, and the massive-walled country villas and farmsteads that went up in the eighteenth century, are beautifully dark and shady.

However, the new anti-seismic building regulations which came into force after the 1968 earthquake in western Sicily meant that developers economised on the increased cost of materials by compressing as many apartments into one block as possible. My flat went up some ten years ago and I am suffering for it. It's attractive enough with balconies and whitewashed walls, but the ceilings are too low and the windows are too large, letting the sun in instead of helping to keep it out.

English people of course love sun-filled rooms. I did too when I first came out here. Before moving in with the two Dublin girls, I was lodging for a week or so with an extraordinary woman in her vast 1920s flat not far from the old centre of Palermo.

The woman who wasn't Sicilian but came I think from Turin, looked like a horse. She was huge, like the rooms in her flat, with an elongated face and shivering jowls which hung in majestic folds under her chin. A widow, probably in her late sixties, she had iron grey hair, wire glasses and an extraordinary dress sense. Her skirts were always dun-coloured and almost down to her black buckled shoes, and she wore loose grey cardigans. But the oddest thing of all about her was the way she washed.

There was of course a bathroom in the house – I can't remember anything about it now, but can easily imagine how it would have been tiled and extremely cold with a claw-footed bath probably on a dais. Anyway, signora Durante didn't use it; she washed in the kitchen sink. I caught her at it one morning and an amazing sight it was.

She had stripped to the waist and was wearing what looked like a sort of calico bodice. I can't think she had a bra on underneath, or if she had, it was definitely what one would have to call a brassière: one of those huge satin affairs bought in the Italian equivalent of Debenham and Freebody's lingerie department. The sink in which she was carrying out her ablutions was, like everything else, massive: a deep, steep-sided stone basin designed for the energetic scrubbing of clothes. But instead of using the tap, signora Durante had taken a bottle of water from the top of a cupboard and was in the throes of pouring the contents over her neck and upper chest. Leaning forward over the sink, legs well apart, she doused her enormous upper limbs in the cold stream, then dried herself with a towel that was so bleached and worn out that it was more like a rag.

I never understood why she chose to wash herself like this, nor why she used the drinking water from one of the supply of bottles she kept on top of the cupboard. There were so many of them up there, all lined up watching us like silent dark-green soldiers.

She was also extremely pious and went to early morning Mass at the heavy baroque church in the nearby tree-shaded square. I used to leave soon after her as I was teaching in a convent at the time, and before going out, if it was a sunny day, would push back the heavy green wooden shutters and fling the tall window wide open. Although the flat was about six feet above street level it was in fact on the ground floor and my bedroom gave straight onto the road; if I leant out I could almost touch the heads of the passers-by. One evening I came home to find signora Durante beside herself.

"What on earth have you done, child?" she burst out as soon as I came in the front door. "Never, *never*, leave the windows open like that again! Terrible, terrible!"

It turned out it wasn't for fear of burglars, but simply that the sun had been blazing into the bedroom all morning bringing a huge crop of dust and flies in with it.

"We never do that here, didn't you know? If you need fresh air, just open the slats of the shutters a crack." She leant forward to show me.

Dust is one of the horrors of the Sicilian housewife, strong sunshine another. The one plays havoc with your soft furnishings, the other with your skin. Like most English people who had been starved for too long of warmth and sunshine, I took no notice. As time went on of course I realised that to be a successful expatriate, you have to observe several basic norms.

All Sicilian dwellings are wisely kept in semi-darkness from late May to October, so an infallible way of spotting the seasoned expatriate is by the luminosity of her house. Pitch darkness from dawn to dusk indicates a very long permanence in Italy indeed; gentle shade from say, 2pm to 6pm, a moderate period, and relentless sunshine all day, a new arrival.

The English on holiday are the worst offenders of all, admitting waves of stifling August air into their hotel rooms from morning till night. Their justification for such a practice seems to be that although it is uncomfortable, it is better to have it now and all in one burst, as there won't be much more of it when they get home.

As well as keeping her house in permanent gloom, the successful expatriate never sweats. Nothing gives the amateur away more easily than a red, perspiring face and corkscrewed clothes. The Englishwoman in the know appears round about 6pm in the summer in crisp cool linen, and will have walked to the open air café to greet her London friends so as not to crease her clothes in the car.

High temperatures are one of the most difficult things to cope with – probably because the Anglo-Saxon body isn't built (unlike the Latin one) to repel excessive heat. The Englishwoman abroad will be careful never to wear rings from June onwards, especially if she is into middle age, as her fingers tend to swell up like sausages. She will also abstain from make-up, for this will run and make her look like an old tart. Something Harold Acton didn't have to contend with, bless him.

"How do you stand it?" we are often asked by visiting countrywomen. "The temperature must be well over a hundred today."

"A hundred? Oh you mean *farenheit!*"

Insisting you don't feel the heat at all, and pretending you now think in

Celsius is another rule to try and keep to. Terribly difficult this last one as no matter how many years the Englishwoman has been out here, she still cannot get inches, feet, pounds and stone out of her system. This is quite logical as the longer she has been away from England, the more likely she is to have been brought up with avoirdupois.

Another giveaway to dilettantism is the over-big ice-cream. No respecting expatriate in the company of others ever orders anything dark-coloured or covered in cream when the temperature is over 30°C (90°F). There is an excellent reason for this. The correct method is to smile politely when her friends ask whether she would recommend the strawberry and coffee cream ice served with dark chocolate sauce, chopped hazelnuts and cream.

"Delicious I should think."

She lifts her eyebrows to the waiter;

"Right then. *Doppio gelato con panna* for both of you? Yes? And for me......a dry martini I think."

"Oh Gay! Go on. Don't let us eat ice creams all on our own!"

"I couldn't possibly at this hour of the day, honestly." I reply, secretly longing for one.

The wisdom of my refusal soon becomes apparent. The seafront wind whips my friends' paper napkins away almost immediately and being English they are loathe to disturb the waiter and ask him to bring another one. The dark chocolate sauce is runnier than they bargained for and begins to drip onto the tablecloth. The ice cream itself, being Italian and made with real strawberries, stains terribly, so when the first blob lands on their clothes, that's it. Worst of all is the brown and pink ring round their mouth they cannot see.

I sip my dry martini and look into the distance.

During the Sicilian summer or late spring, you can expect the fierce hot wind, or *scirocco* (pronounced shi-*rock*-oh) to blow at least once – and probably several more times. It arrives from north Africa across the desert and is extremely unpleasant, scrunching up the flowers and leaving a covering of gritty sand in its wake. You always know it is coming because the sky turns a dull, oppressive yellow, and the leaves and rubbish on the ground start spinning round in worried little vortices.

In the nineteenth century, the nobility would leave their sweltering rooms en masse and take refuge in the "*scirocco* chambers" – cool underground cellars especially built for the purpose – until the wind had passed. I imagine they left the servants to sweat it out above ground and bring down iced sherbets when required.

The *scirocco* can last for up to two days; once I remember, it was so severe and the temperature so high, that birds were dropping exhausted out of the sky. Everyone was angry with everyone else, and we had to dampen the sheets to try and sleep at night. These are the occasions when you curse Italy and everything Italian, send all the bloody expatriate rubbish to hell, and long to be back home. Richmond... Twickenham... the boat race, you think as the sweat pours off. All things cold, damp and mildewed.

The best strategy in the absence of a custom-built *scirocco* chamber, is to seal all the windows and stay indoors until it has passed. The less you move around, the better, and as many Sicilians – especially males – lie down anyway after their midday meal *scirocco* or not, this is no great sacrifice.

I could write a whole book on the afternoon nap or siesta, this absurd and infuriating custom of falling asleep in the middle of the day; it's all so unnecessary and such a waste of time ("just think of all the useful things you could be doing from two to five pm, dear"). One of the reasons in fact the expatriate finds herself unable to conform to the custom of the siesta is the inborn and very English horror of not using her time constructively. In London in the fifties, for instance, you definitely didn't go to the pictures when the sun was out.

"You don't want to go and sit in a stuffy old cinema today," I was told, "get out into the fresh air. You can go to the pictures any day."

Any day meant when it rained, when it was OK to go to museums and things like that. The difference is of course, that in Sicily it's sunny every day, which means that the English person would never get to the cinema at all. Or very rarely. And although she knows very well that it is awful to be outdoors on sweltering summer afternoons – unless she happens to be at the beach – the expatriate will still refuse to admit to the wisdom of the siesta.

But apart from those brief periods of intense heat, don't let's forget how truly wonderful the Mediterranean climate really is. No more frosts, leaden skies or weeks of drizzling rain, no biting east winds, depressing dark winter afternoons, fog or snow. Just short, mild winters, scented, flower-laden springtimes and long, long summers. Here your heating bills are low or non-existent and you'll never have to bother about thick coats, gloves or thermal underwear ever again. And with all this glory goes a body exposed for six months of the year to sunlight and air, a smooth tanned skin, thick glossy hair, a springy, optimistic step. Italians are beautiful, and expatriates want to be that way as well. They don't all succeed of course.

3
Bleeding statues

Long after I had left the Berlitz School and a string of other teaching jobs, I became secretary to H.M. Britannic Consul in Palermo. This was definitely my most prestigious post and the only one – either before or since – at which I received a regular and promptly-paid salary. Things were going really well at last.

But these were the Thatcher years, and in 1980 the British government decided to close down the Palermo office. With package tourism Whitehall felt, Consulates – especially in such backwaters as Sicily – had become redundant. Any business regarding stolen passports, muggings and misfortunes to British nationals (of which there were many) as well as shipping formalities and so on, could be dealt with quite efficiently by single representatives. And Palermo was so very far away, it was hardly worth bothering about – I mean dear, who actually *went* there? So that was the end of a very nice job and its attendant cocktail parties and perks.

By this time I had a Sicilian husband and two children. Things I realised (again recalling West Hampstead NW6), were taking a quite extraordinary turn; I now spoke passably good Italian, had taken my driving test and drove a tubby dark blue Fiat 500 which was to serve me spectacularly well for the next seventeen years.

One of the inevitable consequences of establishing myself abroad of course was not only to lose physical touch with Britain, but also to enter a miasmic no-woman's land where one is neither one thing nor the other. For although I had married an Italian and got citizenship of that country, I kept my British passport. What was I meant to do from now on: be loyal to the country of my birth or embrace the one I was now living in? Nobody seemed to care anything about it either way except me, and in retrospect, perhaps I shouldn't have tortured myself either.

We were married at Hampstead Registry Office where the acting official repeated the ceremony in cringe-making Italian for the benefit of my husband. Just in case he hadn't understood what was going on. I think my newly acquired Italian relatives (none of whom were present) were faintly shocked by our decision to marry abroad, but far too well-bred to say so. However, such defection on our part may have accounted for the ill-assorted collection of presents we got. Unlike most Italian couples, I hadn't made out a wedding list, believing it in the worst possible taste, so obviously got what I deserved. I remember a hideous pea-green candlewick bedspread which the doner – a distant cousin – came in person to lay reverently over our bed.

We moved into a tiny flat in the heart of Palermo in a square officially called Piazza Vittorio Emanuele Orlando but known by everyone as Piazza del Tribunale because of the presence of the Law Courts on one side.

Building of the Law Courts began in the last years of the fascist era, but came to an almost immediate halt on the outbreak of War. Only one flat pilaster of the planned façade managed to be raised to the perpendicular before Italy got caught up in the fighting, and this, together with the blocks of marble (*marmo*) left lying around waiting to be used, earned the square its first name of Piazza Marmi.

Today, a wide flight of stone steps leads up to the white colonnaded facade of this vast, severely symmetrical building. An echoing and intimidating marble interior dwarfs the black and gold toga-clad figures scurrying to and from courtrooms laden with documents. They are pursued by a motley collection of confused, and disenchanted Sicilians driven no doubt to distraction by the slowness of the Italian legal system. A permanent contingent of policemen on the raised forecourt outside can be seen draped over their bright blue and white cars or ferrying magistrates back and forth to the accompaniment of screaming sirens.

The police sirens are one of the sounds I remember most clearly from that period; another is the deep boom and deafening crackle of fireworks. These used to be let off on a particular feastday – it may have been for the patron, Santa Rosalia, or perhaps for some other minor saint – anyway, they were set up in the square, and people would sit all over the Law Court steps to watch them.

Nobody does firework displays like the Italians, and in Palermo they are works of art. These were truly magnificent, starting off fairly modestly and then growing in intensity until the roaring grand finale known in Sicilian as the *masculiata*. The word comes from "masculine", i.e. virile, explosive, orgasmic. The connection is clear: the *masculiata* sets the window frames rattling, lighting up the night sky in a blaze of emerald, scarlet and gold, and finally dying away in a falling shower of sparks.

We used to watch the fireworks from our little sitting room balcony. There was a much better view from up there and anyway the antiquated lift was rather unreliable even if we had wanted to go down into the square. The lift was positioned inside a wrought iron cage and only took-off if you put a ten lire coin into a slot. It was also essential to close the outside gate on each floor with a resounding crash when you got to your front door otherwise nobody else could call it from the other floors. We never seemed to have ten lire to hand which was infuriating, especially as visitors were allowed to ask the *portiera* for a coin, but residents weren't.

Callers to our building were often clients of the lawyer, a large and very handsome grey-haired man living on the third floor, who was highly respected in Palermo. Obviously under considerable stress, they often forgot to close the lift gate properly when they got to his door, which meant that I couldn't get up to our own flat on the top floor.

I suppose Signora Broccolo the *portiera* didn't like to disturb the *avvocato* on the entry phone to ask him to close the lift, so she used another method. She'd call her ancient mother out from the depths of the stuffy old cubby hole where they lived and get her to do it.

"*Mamma, chiama l'ascensore!* – Call the lift!"

This fierce diminutive woman would stand at the base of the lift shaft, hands on hips, head thrown back and screech out:

"The lift! The lift!" until a distant clang was heard and the cage came slowly wheezing downward.

Having hardly any money or furniture, we lived a spartan existence. The flat got very cold in January and February and one of my private students would spend the whole hour of English conversation huddled in her coat. I remember her placing her very expensive leather handbag on my 'coffee table' – a cabin trunk that had come out with me to Sicily and which I had tastefully covered with a sheet of pale blue waxed paper used for lining drawers.

It was about this time that events I had never thought of as having any relevance to myself began easing their way rather uncomfortably into my life. Things like other people's marriages and deaths: Catholic marriages and deaths. And other, extraordinary religious occurrences which had no connection whatsoever with my memories of the dry, tight-lipped, Let Us Pray C.of E. There was the bleeding statue, for instance, which I first read about in the local paper a couple of years ago: a small plaster figure of Christ that had suddenly and quite inexplicably begun to shed blood. The statuette – for it was no more than a foot high – belonged to a family living in a modest and unremarkable suburb of Palermo not far from my own.

Phenomena of this kind are common in Italy, and while I have never taken any real interest, I am still fascinated and disturbed by them. Once such occurrences become known and established as it were by popular consent (although by no means necessarily recognised by the Vatican as miraculous), they nearly always seem to lose their potency. The bleeding or weeping statues and pictures, by now transformed into 'shrines' and places of pilgrimage, literally dry up.

This on the other hand, was a freshly discovered miracle. Apparently – as often happens – this Christ was a cheap statuette, one of thousands like it which are turned out of a plaster cast and sold by the roadside on religious feastdays. Perhaps the family had been on a trip to the holy shrine at Tindari in the east of Sicily or to St. Peter's in Rome, or maybe, who knows, they had had it standing there in the garden for years.

The local newspaper didn't make too much of the story, simply reporting how, on the previous day, the owner of the statue had gone into the garden and caught sight of blood slowly oozing from Christ's eyes. It wasn't long of course before the man's cries brought the rest of the family as well as the next door neighbours running out into the garden to see what had happened. And blood – or something very like it – was indeed emerging in a steady stream from both eyes and dribbling down the Saviour's garments in runnels of scarlet.

Jesus was weeping.

The account gave me a shiver, and still does. I decided to go and see what was happening for myself. Slightly put off by the thought of finding hoards of hysterical women there (I remembered Fellini's grotesque portrait of the miraculously visited children in *La Dolce Vita*), I began by asking a passer-by where the "*statua miracolosa*" was.

He knew, and treated the question as though I had been enquiring after the nearest fishmonger. The Sicilian is far more likely to get excited by the football results than by bleeding statues, and why shouldn't he? Miracles are very definitely in the woman's domain, and one expects mothers, widows and celibate daughters to request God's grace on their menfolks' behalf. You see few males at Italy's holy shrines and sancturies; it is almost as though it were not quite manly to converse with the Creator.

It took a long time to find the house as it was on the outermost perimeter of the suburb. In this area low, jerry-built houses straggled out in untidy and irregular lines over the once open fields. Potholed white dust roads put up a show of connecting them, or petered out at the end of nameless cul-de-sacs. Each house had its own little patch of garden containing more vegetables than flowers, although one or two of the sub-tropical trees that grow all over coastal Sicily had already burst defiantly into spectacular and vivid bloom there. The mountains which surround Palermo on three sides rose up a smoky pink in the distance, and dogs barked frantically behind garden railings.

I had been told to follow "that road" right to its end. And so I did. On it went, shedding its macadamed surface and becoming deeply rutted and weed-choked. It was bordered, as I could now see, by an unusual number of parked cars which because of the uneven surface of the road, appeared to have been flung onto the crests or deep into the troughs of waves. I had obviously arrived.

The house itself lay in a private lane beyond a large remotely controlled gate. As I approached, an elderly crippled woman was being helped over the gate's iron stoop by – perhaps – her daughter. There were three or four of the ugly cement houses on the left and an open field to the right. A small crowd at the end of the lane showed the presence of the house everyone had come to see.

What struck me first was the silence; this is so unusual in any gathering of Sicilians that I thought I must have come to the wrong place. Yet this was it. About twenty or so people were standing motionless in a tiny garden before a small statue on a plinth which was surrounded by banked vases of flowers. Nightlights glowing in their red transparent jackets were set in a semicircle around the statue's feet. All you could hear was collective breathing and the quiet murmured prayers of one of the women as she ran her rosary through her fingers.

I looked up at the statue of Christ and saw a dark brown stain on its front, stretching from the corners of the eyes and running down the length of the body, over the bare feet and onto the plinth. It was a quite extraordinary sight and one which explained the awed and uncharacteristic silence around me.

The owner of the house stood respectfully by as his visitors filed in and out. There was no question whatsoever but that everybody should have the right to see and pray before this miracle, even though a slight but unmistak-

able air of proprietorship showed that this wonderful thing had happened to *him* – that he and his family had been chosen to divulge it.

Later on, this divine gift received a singular and very personal treatment: God's word as it were being interpreted by his disciple. More of that in a moment. For now, the wonder was simply to be observed and pondered.

The next-door neighbours accepted the pilgrimage as something quite natural although it had undoubtedly invaded their privacy. The main gate for instance had to be opened to let cars through for those who couldn't manage the few yards on foot. Yet no one I am sure ever refused them entry or grumbled about the streams of other people who were subsequently to arrive.

When I spoke to the owner, he told me the statue had bled several times more since that first day.

"Just streams out" he said, "look, you can see from the stains."

I never saw the phenomenon take place on any of the three occasions I visited the garden, but the bloodstains are still shockingly present in my mind.

As more and more people came to see the Christ (although the crowds never got anywhere near fanatical proportions), the owner got the idea of adding something of his own. And why not? Taking small wads of cotton wool from a packet, he rubbed them over the bloodstained statue and then put them into a basket. These were then handed out to whoever requested them. Nothing was ever actually said about the wads being available – you just heard that they were.

The cynical – none of whom I ever came across – would have said the cotton wool was handed to pilgrims straight from the pack; it bore no trace at all of red or brown and had no smell. For myself, I have no reason to doubt it had been passed over the plaster Jesus. Even if this hadn't been so, I feel the gesture of *wanting* to share goodness was enough.

Subsequent clinical tests showed that the liquid emanating from the statue was indeed blood, but after a while no more was heard of the Christ and as far as I know no miraculous healings ever took place there.

* * *

Leaving aside miracles and divine intervention, most people of course live a fairly normal existence, living and dying wherever they are in the world. During those first years of marriage though, I seemed to be attending an awful lot of christenings and funerals. The very first I remember, was the death of a very old aunt I barely knew.

As was (and still is) the custom, the front door of the house was left open so that people could come in and pay their respects. The uncovered coffin lay on a bier in the centre of the darkened drawing room with four tall candles in ornate silver candlesticks at each corner. The widower, a diminutive moustachioed man in a heavy black suit and wing collar greeted us formally and then went to sit on his own with bowed head. Among the other mourners sitting around the coffin murmuring quietly with lowered eyes, I noticed the cousin who had given us the nasty candlewick bedspread.

I had had nothing suitable to wear for the wake and had to borrow a black polo-necked jumper of Franco's. It was thick wool, much too hot and scratched horribly.

"Should I............?" I whispered as we came in.

On arrival, one was expected to go up to the body, look into its face or say a short prayer of farewell. This is particularly trying as the jaw is tied up with a white cloth so that it won't gape in death. Trying to conceal your disquiet as you bend over is difficult.

It was no mark of disrespect that after some time, the mourners began to chat softly amongst themselves about other matters as they sat round the catafalque. This helped to fill in time before the arrival of the undertakers. And arrive they did very soon afterwards with loud banging of doors and raised voices.

No respect seems to be shown – or even expected – from Palermo undertakers. They are men getting on with a job and as such, usually turn up in their working clothes of jeans and shirtsleeves. Worst of all is the din they make nailing or sealing down the coffin lid and then manouevring the whole thing through doorways and down flights of stairs which are invariably too narrow.

I watched all this in disbelief – especially the way the male mourners took such a fascinated interest in the mechanics of the operation. You felt they would have liked to have a go of the oxyacetylene flame themselves.

There is no cremation yet in Palermo which makes for gruesome overcrowding in cemeteries. The increase in the urban population has done away with the elaborate funerals I used to see in the sixties when the body would be decorously borne away in a glass-sided carriage drawn by four black plumed horses. The humbler the family, the greater the accompanying pomp. Now, the cortège can hardly get moving from the church or the house for the traffic, and there's just a utilitarian hearse (with or without metal cross on top), a van transporting the wreaths, and an undignified jumble of mourners.

Tradition dictates that the mourners follow the hearse on foot; they probably used to go all the way to the cemetery, but nowadays can only manage a couple of hundred yards. At the funeral of an elderly trade union leader I went to recently, we found ourselves in the midst of a very unholy traffic jam. The hearse had somehow managed to cut a path through snorting hooting cars and buses, leaving us straggling behind.

A religious ceremony was out of the question as the deceased had been a communist of the old school, so a secular spoken tribute of some sort had to be delivered. The cemetery where he was to be buried was in a village outside the city; it was now or never.

The task fell to the most prominent mourner present: a Sicilian member of Parliament and comrade of the deceased. Stopping suddenly in the middle of the road so that we all tripped over one another, he held up his hand.

"It is up to me to say a few words about......."

Whatever these words were I never knew, as they were immediately swallowed up in the roar of a passing lorry. I watched his mouth opening and shutting in fascinated disbelief. This can't be true I thought; this can't be me standing here in the middle of one of Palermo's busiest intersections breathing in exhaust fumes and listening to a tribute.

"...with such courage and fortitude.."

People were craning their necks behind car windows a few inches away to get a better look at our little group. The driver of the hearse in front stuck his head out.

"Has he nearly finished?" he bellowed, "we can't stay here all night."

"........always true to his principles," the M.P. continued doggedly, "an honest and committed member......... a tragic loss to all....."

He was drowned out, and as soon as was decently possible we all fled.

Grotesque funerals like this are only one aspect of the problem, lack of consecrated ground is another. For while the birth rate in the country is now zero, deaths evidently continue to occur at a spanking pace. Even the privately-owned mausolea which many Palermo families built for themselves, are sooner or later going to fill up. But that's another story and far too gruesome to go into here. Suffice to say that cremation, legalised in England almost a hundred years ago in 1902, is not yet on the cards in Palermo.

I admit to being fascinated by all the rituals of passing into the next world, and actually enjoy visiting cemetries, the more ornate and bizarre the better. One raw October day we decided to visit the grave of the bandit Salvatore Giuliano – or Turriddu as he was known – whose grave is in the cemetery, set above the mountain village of Montelepre about thirty-five kilometers from Palermo.

"WE WERE LIKE YOU" is written depressingly over the entrance gate, "YOU WILL BE LIKE US".

I asked a keeper moodily stabbing at some weeds where the grave was located, and he pointed silently with his hoe.

"Up that way?" I asked indicating an avenue gloomy with cypresses stretching away into the distance.

He nodded, laid the hoe aside and began cleaning out his ear with the crucifix dangling from the chain round his neck.

Salvatore Giuliano was forced to flee Montelepre where he had been born in 1922, after killing a *carabiniere*. For the next seven years or so, up until 1950, he and his band of *picciotti* or henchmen, lived as outlaws in the wild and inhospitable surrounding mountains. Good-looking, courageous and shrewd, Giuliano became the romantic folk of the time, the champion of the desperately poor and oppressed Sicilian *contadini,* staging a series of hold-ups, kidnappings and robberies. Anybody driving up into those mountains did so at their peril.

As a small boy, my husband Franco remembers having the bandit pointed out to him one day in a Palermo street, wearing his characteristic white raincoat and high leather boots. To have come down into the city at all was a sign of the power he commanded at the time.

Giuliano's connections with the Mafia and the Sicilian Separatist Movement of the time began to get the Centre-Right wing government seriously rattled, and it was decided he would have to go. Gaspare Pisciotta, his cousin and the member of the band closest to him, was persuaded to carry out the killing, no doubt on the promise of leniency once the men had been rounded up. Murdering Giuliano, however, was not going to be an easy task as the bandit never went anywhere without his shotgun. Pisciotta accordingly put a sleeping draught into his cousin's drink and when he was comatose, shot him.

Once the deed was done, it had to appear the work of the strong and able government's highly efficient police force. So the body was secretly taken to another part of the town of Castelvetrano and a mock shoot-out staged. He was laid out in a courtyard and photographed surrounded by armed *carabinieri,* and this was the official account served up to Italians of the bandit's end.

The story doesn't end here, as the unfortunate supergrass Pisciotta, predictably thrown into gaol together with the rest of the band and outraged at his own betrayal, threatened to tell all. Enter, and not for the first time, the Mafia. Pisciotta's father also in prison, was ordered by Cosa Nostra to silence his son with a cup of poisoned coffee. This dreadful act was duly done and the whole affair goes to show – if one was not already aware of the fact – just how well-cemented the collusion was between Mafia and State and how overriding the power of the former.

As the Palace of Justice (in the square where I was later to live) was still unfinished in 1953, part of the trial of Giuliano's band was held in the Court of Appeal set up in the deconsecrated church of Santa Maria di Montevergini in Palermo. This is in one of the oldest and most desperately poor areas of the city, the Capo, a labyrinth of filthy alleyways and crumbling tenements. Although the whole area had been cordoned off, the *carabinieri* allowed children from the nearby school to duck under the ropes and get into class. Franco, who was one of those pupils has never forgotten seeing the prisoners arriving at the court, handcuffed to iron rods and chained together by their ankles. Herded out of the police van like animals, they were made to shuffle up the steps and into the court.

After half an hour's wandering along the damp cemetery paths we still hadn't found Giuliano's tomb. The rows of mausolea and private chapels belonging to the more monied local families rose one beside the other, sometimes so close together that there was barely room to pass between them. It was deathly quiet. Then turning a corner at the end of one of the avenues, we came upon a little group of people – the first we had seen so far. They seemed to be cleaning-up – sweeping, putting fresh flowers in vases and so on. The gate to the vault they were seeing to stood open and looking in I could see its dismal, semi-umbral interior.

"Let's ask them where Giuliano's tomb is" I said, "they're bound to know."

They certainly were, but we could hardly ask because as we got nearer we noticed the family name written in cubital letters over the lintel of the vault: PISCIOTTA.

Family feuds take a very long time – if ever – to heal in Sicilian village life, and one as tragic and dramatic as this will probably continue for many years to come. It would have been the height of bad taste to ask Pisciotta's relatives where Giuliano lay.

Actually, it was almost next door. If you go there, you will find the door left standing open rather as though it were public shrine. Which perhaps it is. A small oval-shaped photograph and short inscription shows which is Salvatore's tomb.

Coming back down the winding road from Montelepre you get a dramatic view of these fierce bare, mountains, rent in places by distant brilliant patches of sea and one or two clusters of tiny villages. Village is not really the right description for these at all, but then neither is town. The first gives the idea of a handful of picturesque cottages gathered round a village green (which they are definitely not), and the second is far too urban with its connotations of buses and a High Street. What in fact most of the Sicilian *paesi* are, is a straggled-out line of dwellings often built on different levels with a central square, terrible roads and several churches.

And my God, what a lot of churches there are in Sicily – the island fairly groans with them. During my first few years here, their imposing ornate interiors left me dazzled; they were "masterpieces... glorious.... amazing.. incredible.. stupendous". As time went by and more and more of them were added to my itineraries, they became "interesting..pleasant...quite attractive"; now, after so long, they are simply "nice" or "OK".

The Catholic mass which I have never been able to identify with, is still, I am afraid to admit, achingly boring to me, with ceremonies such as christenings and confirmations being quite excruciating in their lengthiness. I honestly wonder whether anyone – Italian or otherwise – is able to sit rapt through a seemingly endless First Communion.

Not that Church of England services are any better. I remember being bored almost beyond endurance by the lessons and sermons when I was a child. And things haven't changed there either. Visiting the London church of All Saints in Margaret Street not long ago, I felt the awful monotony creeping over me again. All Saints is very High Church with services virtually indistinguishable from those in Italy – except for the one startling differ-

ence of the rigidly silent English congregation. (Continentals do make such a noise in church, don't you know.) The dynamics too differ slightly, with the Sicilian priest favouring a microphone rather than the correct projection of his voice. Perhaps disliking such a worldly artifact, he tends to place it much too near his mouth, thus transforming the gentle augury *il Signore sia con voi* – may the Lord be with you – into a threatening roar.

The All Saints congregation was well-heeled and with a suprisingly strong male contingent. I was really there to look at the church's architecture and just happened to arrive when Mass was in progress. At the end, to my great astonishment, instead of rushing home to Sunday lunch, everyone gathered in the little courtyard for sherry.

Now this must be one of those classic examples of living in a time warp: I had no idea that this was what went on in English churches. Sherry? In fact I was so taken aback that I persuaded the friend who was with me that we should get a glass too. For some reason I never imagined we'd have to pay for it. Of course we did. "This is meant to be a friendly get-together" my friend who spent a great deal of time in London said, "a lot of the churches do it now". Be that as it may, nobody talked to or took the slightest notice of us. The only smile I got was when I handed over my pound notes to the lady behind the drinks table. We finished our exorbitantly priced sherry and slunk away.

This doesn't seem a very Christian or charitable atmosphere to me, but of course I may be wrong. The fact that a flowery dressed lady in the little adjacent shop was doing a very nice trade in pomanders and home-made jams does make me think, however. What came first I wonder, the Pope John Paul II ashtray or the All Saints Margaret Street teatowel?

4
Handsome men, beautiful women

A visiting Englishman I spoke to years ago was absolutely floored by Sicilian male youth:

"They're so *slim*!" he breathed.

So slim is not a way I would immediately describe them myself, although I suppose they are less bumpy than their English counterparts. This has a lot to do with clothes, for the fewer you have to wear, the smoother you are going to appear. The visiting Englishman was gay and contemplating beauty from his particular viewpoint. He'd never have used the word "slim" otherwise. But other comments I have heard over the years have been just as odd.

One person wanted to know why Italian men were always touching their crotches, another pointed out how they spat all the time, another asked why they congregated in the village squares; Englishwomen too say they can't understand why the men *stare* so much. I bet they can't.

Do the Italians really bother to wonder in the same way about Englishmen? I'm quite sure they don't. We are terribly critical as a race: why, why do the Italians do this or that, why don't they do it our way? One thing not in question though is Latin beauty: a different kind to our own, and very much in evidence, especially, down here in the south.

It's interesting that in English romantic novels the hero is always tall, dark and handsome whereas in Italian 'Mills and Boons' he is blond with blue eyes. Why each race should see the other's stereotypical male as ideal, I don't really know.

Advertisements too on Italian television invariably show golden-haired children and delicately complexioned housewives – not a dark one among them. Funny.

Blond is evidently beautiful and sells toilet rolls and mineral water.

"Look here Gino, when we had the swarthy Sicilian guy doing water biscuits, sales went down by 30%. We really can't afford to make mistakes like that again. Get a flaxen-haired bambino from the Milan agency or you're out."

"But Vittorio, you said black designer stubble was just what you wanted..."

"Not any more. I'm through with hairy forearms and flashing eyes. People want sweetness and light now. Sweetness and light.....get it? They want cornfields and waterfalls, all that back-to-nature crap. Fat mammas and weatherbeaten old fishermen are out; they don't sell a damn thing."

No visitor to Italy can fail to notice how the races vary throughout the peninsular. South of Rome for instance, you get the olive-skinned, black-haired, dark-eyed Mediterranean, north of the capital are the slightly taller Alpine people with brown hair and brown eyes, while in the Veneto and Friuli regions, the dominant strain is Dinaric or slightly slav- looking. Everywhere up north, you find the tall, fair nordic type, while the Sicilian, as mentioned earlier, is a mixture, thanks to his Greek, Arab, Norman and Iberian ancestors.

For a year or so I lived in Umbria, the small central region known as the green heart of Italy, which although delightfully calm and beautiful, has unremarkable-looking people. The men there tend to have mournful countenances and drooping moustaches and wear loden overcoats and tweedy fishermen's hats with down-turned brims; the women are rather solidly built and ruddy-complexioned. They weren't in fact what the English usually imagine as "typically Italian" at all. Down here on the other hand, people are exactly as you expect them to be: predominantly dark with strong-features, good teeth and shiny hair. They are stylishly-dressed, graceful of movement and beautiful. Of course you get the runts – where in the world wouldn't you? The ghastly old crone (which is what I shall probably be myself one day), and the leering, greasy-haired youth head a whole contingent of carbuncle-encrusted noses, hooded eyes, loose blubber lips, dirt-engrained hands and smelly bodies. The glory of variety.

Yet when I go out in the morning in Palermo, even the road sweepers, policemen and the bus drivers look handsome to me. It's all to do with my London childhood. In those days bus drivers were solidly-built men in their fifties – ordinary, homely and dreadfully uninspiring. Even if you could see them at all behind the dark-brown concertinered curtain that shut them off from the rest of the number 159 bus, you'd certainly never associate them with romantic longings. It was the same with our street cleaners and policemen: dully uniformed and utilitarian. Evenin' all, just doing my beat. What time is it? Six o'clock Madam. Here on the other hand, the metropolitan police have gorgeous slim-fitting uniforms and are exceedingly sexy. They notice, rather than ignore the women. Even Mildred gets a flutter when she comes. Especially if its a scarlet and black-clad *carabiniere* on horseback with a gleaming sword by his side.

The expatriate of course pretends not to notice the overwhelming attractiveness of the police, preferring to criticise their inefficiency like the Italians themselves do. The other morning driving through the Favorita – a large wooded park which connects the city to its coastal suburbs, I saw two mounted officers leaning down and talking to a couple of the prostitutes who ply their trade in the park. Getting them to move on I suppose.

These women either sit on carboard boxes facing the oncoming traffic with their legs wide open, or stand by the roadside, fat thighs emerging from rucked-up mini-skirts. Motorists see them suddenly as they come racing out of a bend in the road, so if a man wants their services, he has to slow down and draw into the grass verge. Apart from being terribly dangerous to the cars following behind, this is only the start, for the prospective client will now have to occupy roadspace for an even longer period as he agrees on a tariff.

I used to play tennis on a municipal court in another part of the Favorita where it was perfectly safe to park. Every time I got out of my car, I used to see the raddled old *poule* whose patch that particular lay-by was. In her midfifties, she was the most awful ragbag you have ever seen, and used to rest her poor varicosed legs by sitting on a filthy boulder and waiting for clients. And clients she must have had, for the boulder was often vacated when I returned from my game, and a little three-wheeled van parked nearby.

I never quite knew how to acknowledge her presence; whether by a curt nod of the head or a tight, superior smile, or whether indeed I should show I had noticed her at all. One day the lay-by was rather full and I had to put the car near her boulder. As I was shutting the door and walking away, she called me back.

"Look, couldn't you park a bit further away? I have to work, you know."

Now, what does the snooty Englishwoman from N.W.6 answer in cases like this?

"My good woman" (perhaps), "you have no right to be here in the first place, and I shall leave my car exactly where I choose. Good morning to you."

or:

"How dare you! Who do you think you are? I shall report you to the appropriate authorities immediately."

Of course, all I did say, being thoroughly feeble was:

"Yes, I'm so sorry, I'll move it at once."

I can't imagine the prostitutes are allowed by law to occupy the *Favorita*, yet I have never seen them rounded up by those mounted police who occasionally patrol its roads. In fact, by the time I returned some two hours later that other morning, both ladies and police had disappeared. *Carabinieri* on whoresback perhaps?

But I am digressing. This was going to be about Latin loveliness. I would like to have been as beautiful as Gina Lollobrigida when I was thirteen years old; she seemed to me to have such very perfect features. Seeing her only the other day on television, I can vouch she still looks every bit as good, which is more than you can say of the terrifyingly aggressive Sophia Loren. Mind you, you don't say nasty things about Loren, especially not in front of the middle-aged Italian male, as she is considered a *mito* or legend in the cinema to them. It was a big surprise to me though when she went and married little Carlo Ponti (Charles Bridges). I couldn't help thinking she could have had the most gorgeous man in the world if she'd wanted to.

I have always admired Italian women's chic and the fact they can even look good in glasses. I never did when I had to wear them. Ageing Italian actresses on the other hand, realise that huge tinted spectacles can be an asset; they nearly all wear them here: Sophia Loren, Claudia Cardinale... I always try to look behind the lenses to discover whether the lines and crows' feet are still there or have been surgically smoothed away. Turbans too are skilfully adopted; there's a sixty-something stage actress, for instance, who never appears in public without this swathe of silk wound round and round her head and coming low down over her eyes like some demented snail.

You can't comfortably wear tinted glasses in England, the light's too muted. Anyway, imagine Emma Thompson say, in a massive pair of smoky-blue specs. Or Maggie Smith in a turban. They don't care enough. And that's the main difference between the females of both races: Italian women are far more loath to throw in the towel than we are.

I suppose the little black-clad women the tourists so love to seek out in Italian villages, never had towels in the first place to throw in. Hard to imagine *them* entrusting themselves to the plastic surgeon, and anyway their myriad-lined faces for some reason are always considered wonderful, marvellous, full of character. I try to show them off when I have English visitors.

"Quick Mildred, over there! There's one of them just disappearing into that hovel. Did you see her?"

"Missed her I'm afraid. What I'm really after is one carrying an urn on her head."

"There! Over there! Just turning the corner. Oh surely, you saw her this time?"

"Afraid not, dear. I thought you said Sicilian villages were full of little black women. I must admit I'm rather disappointed. Now when I was in Florence in the....."

"Oh for heaven's sake! It's not my fault if you keep missing them: the place is fairly buzzing with black...."

"And the donkeys. You said we'd see peasants on donkeys carrying bundles of hay, and we haven't come across one all morning."

The expatriate is eager to point out Mediterranean beauty in all its forms: the sophisticated urbane charm of its city population and the picturesque earthiness of its peasants in the countryside and villages. Quite mad of course. You wouldn't dream of photographing the inhabitants of Great Missenden or Long Crendon. Or would you? Yes, I suppose that is just what some Italian tourists do.

Italian girls are graceful when they walk and when they sunbathe on the beach, but there again, they've got the climate on their side: if you know you'll be wearing a bikini all summer, you see to it your figure is in trim. Not like the English who go straight from cool Spring to boiling Mediterranean summer and buy a swimming costume at Marks at the last moment. The body just can't take it.

Italians know how to lie on the beach and look good: straight-limbed and perfectly still. They have clean, fluffy towels and the right sort of sun cream which comes out of pots not tubes. They get up slowly and always let their hair get wet when they go in the sea so that it's black and gleaming and clinging to the back of their neck when they come out. My swimming at Bexhill-on-Sea was a rubber bathing cap with a strap under the chin, no sun at all, and an agonising shingle beach. Looking good didn't come into it; it was a dash for the windbreak and a warm sweater when you came out of the water. I think that's probably why I have never converted successfully to Mediterranean sophistication. My sun cream is still gritty for instance and I still do the breast stroke with my head sticking out of the water.

None of this, however, is in evidence when English visitors arrive, and the expatriate is quite likely to dive under the surface of the water oblivious of her hair, or heave herself playfully onto a floating raft with the natives. "Come on out, it's *lovely!*"

Sicilian men look even better in swimming trunks. Up to a certain age of course, one can't expect miracles. Funnily enough, although they're islanders, they're not great swimmers and prefer just lying or draping themselves around the seascape. As they don't have to bother about getting a tan – being already nice and swarthy. It must get rather boring for them sometimes.

A great deal of rather infantile activity is indulged in to kill this monotony; one of the most idiotic is *tamburello*, a game played on the sands by two people hitting a plastic ball back and forth with tambourines. There seems to be no score or skill in it whatsoever, just a dull *boy-ing boy-ing boy-ing*, hour after hour after hour. Admittedly, it is a game played by the unlovely and the charmless (the kind of people Franco graphically describes as wankers in the vestry), and as such, need not over-concern us here.

The really gorgeous man on the other hand, spends a long time preening and displaying his body. You hate to look but can't help it: the smooth oiled skin and hard well-exercised limbs, the thin gold chain round the neck and the impeccable haircut. He wouldn't play *tamburello* if you paid him. Every fifteen minutes or so, he will rise from his snow-white towel, remove his sunglasses, stride elastically to the end of the jetty and dive cleanly into the sea. No Englishman could handle his narcissism with such panache.

We have rented the same bathing hut at the beach for years now: a simple wooden cube set on a flat rock overhanging a crystal-clear sea. Although Sicily is an island and you can, in theory, go anywhere you like to swim, the best solution if you have to stay in town during the summer, is to rent a pad on a nearby privately owned piece of coast. Scandalously undemocratic as this is, it nevertheless guarantees you three glorious months of sun and sea bathing without the company of used nappies, dogshit or blaring radios.

Yet I still gets a twinge each time I pass the packed public beach. It looks so very hot there and so very crowded. These are Palermo's unlovely and underpriviledged families: not charming, not graceful but defiantly and uncaringly fat, happy, untidy and noisy. Every inch of sand is covered in bodies, plastic picnic bags, collapsible chairs and tables, shrieking children. "They look perfectly happy to me, dear, I can't see what you're worrying about" Mildred says, "oh do look at that delightful tot with the ice lolly; what a happy little fellow he is! Anyway, I dare say they'd spoil your lovely clean beach if they could get their hands on it".
Mm.

* * *

At least they were cool and wet there on the beach. Water is an extremely precious commodity in Sicily. Three reservoirs in the surrounding hills around Palermo supply the city, while an antiquated and leaky mains system carried it to its houses. Things have always been ghastly as far as supply and distribution go, yet everyone always claims the island has plenty of water, and that shortages have nothing to do with rainfall. Apparently, although many of the rivers have dried up over the years, the undergound springs are still there and anywhere you sink a well, so they say, you are bound to strike lucky. Except that it's illegal to drill for water and – again as everybody tells you – its the Mafia who control the existing wells and decides who is and who isn't to benefit.

"Listen to me, my good man, I demand access to your well immediately" is not guaranteed to bring results even if you are the Law.

Like a lot of other people, our solution has been to instal a 1000 litre tank high on the outside wall of our flat as an emergency supply. Not high enough unfortunately as the balcony above is only 2 metres 70 overhead and as the water falls by gravity alone, we only get the feeblest of trickles in the taps.

One of the most terrible things that can happen is for the mains water supply to dry up or be cut off without warning in the middle of summer. This gets quite atrocious when the expatriate has guests, especially if these are elderly, terribly English, or both.

"How do you put up with it, Gay? I'd go quite mad."

"Don't, it's awful. Luckily we've got the tank."

But the tank hasn't the strength to flush the lavatories which, when they are in perfect working order, evacuate their contents by means of a tremendously fierce pressure valve. I wonder now how I used to put up with the English wall cistern with its one ladylike and totally inadequate flush. Here, the water roars through the steel pipes for as long as you choose. When everything's gone, you throw the handle and switch off.

However, when the Mains are off in Palermo, buckets of water have to be brought in and emptied into the lavatory pan. The flat is like a tenement in no time with old floor cloths set around to catch the drips, jugs for carrying to and fro, and bottles of mineral water put next to the basin to wash your teeth with.

If you telephone the water company on such occasions and demand why nothing is coming through the taps, you will be told (if they answer at all) there is a *guasto* (pronounced *gwast*-oh) or breakdown.

"There's a *guasto* Signora." Never anything else.

Although such disasters deal a terrible blow to the expatriate's prestige, she can, if skilful, still clamber back. Experience in fact, has shown that when the water finally does return, the relief felt by all is so great, that the incident is soon forgotten.

"Everyone to the lav!" she calls, whipping the cloths off the bathroom floor. Make a joke of it.

"Oh! what a heavenly sound, dear. I think I'll take a shower and maybe wash out a few smalls. May I be the first?"

Drinks all round, bougainvillea watered, dishwater and washing machine pounding away... perhaps it wasn't so bad after all.

But it was. Things were never like this in England. Never. If it's one thing that will send me back to Britain it will be the Sicilian water shortage. It makes you mean, spying on the neighbours to see if they sluice down their terrace too often.

How did Harold cope, I wonder. Quite certainly he would never have endangered his status and image by letting the taps run dry on his guests; that would have been unthinkable. It is one thing after all to show off charming Italian customs and picturesque servants to your literary friends but quite another to expect them to flush their own shit away with a plastic bucket.

There was no water the other day at the tennis club I belong to. Normally the courts are hosed down before you play: a graceful arc of sparkling droplets turning the surface a deep terracotta and bringing out the scent of wet earth, jasmine and oleander bushes. This time though it was like playing in a desert; the dust flying up into our faces and turning our whites brick-red. This was especially annoying as earlier that morning I had been to buy new socks and underwear.

"I want some tennis knickers please," I said to the woman in the shop. The shop was part of a chain of very old-fashioned drapers which have been going in Palermo for as long as I remember. Totally devoid of chic, they cater almost exclusively for dowdy thick-ankled matrons and men in cardigans. However, they also stock most of the well-known brands of women's underwear.

The shop assistant opened a box and showed me an appalling pair of Y-fronts.

"I can't wear those" I said, "they're for men."

"No, Signora, they're ladies' tennis knickers. Look, it says so on the box."

And indeed it did. The dreadful garment came right up to the waist; it was out of the question.

"What about a bra, Signora? They do a special tennis one too."

Predictably, this was all rubber and very strong cotton, and again, quite impossible. That was why I was playing in totally unsuitable lacy pants the morning the water was off. Not that it mattered, for the club is normally frequented at that time by elderly white-haired men who are wholly committed to their game. Wiry and energetic, they leap alarmingly about the court, the sweat streaming from their faces, taking no notice whatsoever of the other players. Sometimes they leap extra high and fall over, but it never stops their game.

Reddened and exhausted after our match, I got home to find the water was off there too.

"You can travel all over the world" Mildred always says "but you'll never find anywhere as good as England". She seems so right in moments like these.

5
Flora and fauna

Not long ago I went to an exhibition of photographs on Palermo's fruit and vegetable market. The stark black and white pictures had all been taken in the same market in the fifties and early sixties and showed buyers and sellers, half-starved dogs and poor bulbous cauliflowers, potatoes and root fennel piled high on the ground. There were lorryloads of cabbages, and a sea of donkey carts jostling for space; there were nuns oblivious to the camera clutching purses, a policeman in peaked cap and crumpled khaki looking on, a few sharp-eyed women craning their necks over people's backs. There were brass scales held aloft, an urn bubbling away on the crumb-strewn counter of an early morning coffee stall.

The men in the photographs were short, dark-skinned and clumsily-featured with bewildered staring eyes and black hair swept straight back from low foreheads. They looked 'earthern', with jackets and trousers darned here and there with pieces of wire thread. Some had bent strips of cigarettes in their mouths, and some wore the typical Sicilian flat cap or *coppola*. Their pathetic rags and expressions of resigned wretchedness made me want to weep. Yet at the same time the realisation that they have gone for good was startling.

You just don't see people like these any more; the *contadini* who soon after these pictures were taken began leaving the villages and moving into Palermo or emigrating abroad, got jobs, ate more nutritious food and over the years gave rise to a different looking person altogether. In wartime Britain it was the fashions and hair styles that made our parents look so different and I am sure that if you blotted these out and superimposed modern clothes on them, the people would appear completely up-to-date. But you can't do this with the Sicilian because something inside has gone.

A lot of Palermo's original inhabitants, probably most of them, see this lost quality – almost the disappearing gene – as a precious one, and as society being worse off for having let it slip away. It has various names: integrity, honesty, a sense of the family and, although nobody would dream today of voicing it, a sense of (horrors) "knowing one's place". By the late 1960s and 1970s this new Sicilian held relatively little interest for the aristocracy which has never enjoyed a very prestigious image down here anyway or gone out of its way to better the peasants' lot. Besides, the various counts and princes themselves were well into decline by now. The new Sicilian presence was felt more by the urban middle classes, and had I suppose consequences in some ways similar to those of the Industrial Revolution in England.

In spite of all this upheaval – of the Sicilians getting taller, healthier, better off and better educated – lots of things stayed the same. They were still an ebullient and volatile people, and in many ways still very conventional in outlook and behaviour. Putting this more simply, all it means is that my next-door neighbours shout and laugh a lot and very loudly but can be almost prim about the morality of their daughters.

Sicilians still love good food but are not great wine consumers; they enjoy being in each others' company but are not particularly fond of open air pursuits or sports. They like their cars and they keep their houses excruciatingly clean and tidy, but don't really care how dirty their streets and public gardens get. They seem to have a high tolerance level as far as noise goes and are loath to complain about blaring music or screaming neighbours; in fact I believe they find silence a horrible and rather frightening state to be in. Totally unable (or perhaps, unwilling) to organise themselves, they have an intense dislike of any form of discipline, or of laws or rules being imposed upon them, yet they are fanatical about the dos and don'ts of the social rites within their own families.

This of course could go on and on and get very boring for anyone who has never been to southern Italy or met any of its inhabitants, and who never intends to come anyway; yet it does give an idea of some of the differences between us. If you repeat that last paragraph for instance substituting the English for the Sicilians, I think you'd find we were the direct opposite. And that can make for quite a bit of friction.

I didn't add to that list by the way that animals and plants are not particularly liked down here – a quite outrageous state of affairs and one that the Englishwoman does all in her power to counteract. My fanatically cultivated balcony is a source of bemused wonder to a lot of those who see it. Very nice (and of course she's *foreign*), but why exactly does she do it – I mean, all that work and time.... why not just put a cactus in a pot against the railing and be done? Of course one could do that, but cacti grow to obscene proportions out here, and the less you water them, the more tenaciously they survive. There is nothing charming or ornamental at all about an outsize *euphorbia caneriensis* cactus crawling disgustingly up the outside of a block of flats.It is common knowledge after all that plants grow much bigger in the Mediterranean and that this is nothing whatsoever to do with the skill of the gardener. Still, I try to get people to notice them.

"You should see those geraniums Mildred, great *bushes* of them; just growing wild," I say.

"I know dear, I was in Florence myself before the war. Staying with Harold actually."

"No, no, I'm talking about *Sicily* – the flowers down there, you've just no idea...."

"There were these wonderful *datura* down by the pool; thorn apples you know. Oh, the scent! Quite overpowering. I remember Winston remarking on their...."

"Oh my goodness me, I've seen scores of those, they grow like weeds down in Taormina. No, what you should see are those enormous rubber trees they have growing in Palermo: quite extraordinary plants; unique in fact. They've got these great aerial roots and thick, thick trunks, and the other roots you know spread for miles underneath the......"

"I don't think I'd take to those at all, Gay. Shut out all the light. No, no, what I remember so vividly in Florence are the clouds of jasmine all over the pergolas in the garden, just like gossamer it was.... Edith and Osbert did so love to fool around with it: picking sprigs of it off and putting it in each others' hair! Ah dear, all so very long ago...... "

One of the drawbacks of mass tourism (the Industrial Revolution again) is that nothing is news anymore in the Mediterranean; everything's been observed, plumbed and exploited. And that includes its flora. Now that you can grow grapes and bougainvillea in England, there's not much fun any more seeing them in their natural setting here. There may be headier scents in the gardens in the evening in Sicily, and bigger blooms, but there are also bigger and nastier insects. I'm quite put to it sometimes to come up with something original to show people.

This is all a great pity as Palermo has one of the finest botanical gardens in the world: a wonderful horticultural hotchpotch where such worldly things as turnstiles or societies of "Friends of the Palermo Botanical Garden" would be quite unthinkable. Nobody seems to go there anyway except a for handful of tourists. Entrance is free and timetabled with characteristic eccentricity.

Set on one side of a deafening main road which sweeps down to the sea, the gardens are entered by a narrow gate which for some reason is never fully opened so that you have to ease yourself in sideways. I always feel the custodian sitting morosely on a dining room chair just inside resents your presence and wishes you hadn't bothered to come in the first place.

Palm trees of every species have been growing here since the gardens were planted out over a hundred years ago, their fronds waving gently way above your head. An elegant avenue of these leads to the great lily pond whose waters coil thickly about goldfish and lotus blossoms. Round the edge of the pool are groves of bamboo and there are cool stone seats where you can sit quietly and watch the scarlet damselflies darting over the surface.

This huge and tangled paradise contains such extraordinary trees as the false kapok which has a bulbous thorn-covered trunk and rock-hard seed pods the size of small bananas. Or you can wash you hands with the fruits of the soap tree whose small olive-like berries fall to the ground with little "thuts" and produce a soft white lather when moistened. These and other wonders which seem to be more or less left to their own devices are only a part of this untamed secret garden.

"The curator of Kew would die of apoplexy if things were done as casually at Kew as they are at Palermo" remarked one astounded English traveller in 1901. He was referring to the way rare plants were allowed to share their plots with a cheerful profusion of weeds, and how visitors like himself were left free to lop off bits of bourgainvillea or anything else that took their fancy.

Not a lot has changed really since then; busts of disgruntled-looking benefactors and past curators may stare sternly down from their plinths but no notices caution you to keep to the paths; wild flowers still abound in the beds and succulent grapefruit continue to fall to the ground and rot there; I have helped myself more than once to these and to the oranges and lemons which nobody else seems interested in picking up.

From time to time, the academic staff get together and a new set of brochures or another lavishly illustrated book on the garden is produced.

I was involved in one such venture, having translated the latest oeuvre containing the history of the gardens and the complete catalogue of its specimens. It was hard to imagine who this huge glossy tome was addressed to, being far too heavy and shiny to hold comfortably and rather too scientific to be of interest to the lay reader.

The book in which both English and Italian texts appeared, was launched one morning in the lecture room in the Botanical Garden buildings. I had dressed carefully for the occasion although I came fairly low down in the heirarchy of the production team and didn't expect to be actively involved in the proceedings. This doesn't mean that mine had been an easy task; on the contrary, it had been quite horrific: over a year's work with thousands of Latin botanical names, and an uncomfortable working relationship with the publishers.

I had secreted myself modestly halfway down the hall while the co-authors and publisher took their places on the platform, when to my surprise and dismay, I heard my name:

"... who undertook the translation, not only of the entire text, but of all the captions to the illustrations, and the index: a truly herculean task. We should like her to come up and (laugh laugh) explain how an English person could possibly choose to live and work in this fraught island of ours and how she ....."

This is an old chestnut and one which demands a fairly standard response, but in this case I was also expected to add something about the difficulties of translating botanical texts. Several possibilities went through my mind as I walked up to the platform: I could for example tell them of the dreadful row I had had with the director of the publishing company who wanted to pay me on completion of the work. No foreign writer in her right mind working in Italy ever accepts such an arrangement as it spells professional penury. I had insisted – amid incredulous expostulations – on receiving payment for each instalment of the translated text I handed over. That or nothing doing. I won.

"I am asked" I began now as the television cameras zoomed in on me "to explain how an English person finds life in Italy" (here we go again), "and how I went about translating this beautifully produced book."

Nobody was the slightest bit interested and I had nothing prepared anyway. It was better to get it over with as soon as possible.

"Believe it or not, there are several factors which link the English and the Sicilians: our love of plants for instance" (absolute rubbish) "We, like you, are extremely attached to our local flora and our parks. Kew Gardens which you will all have heard of...."

And so it went on, my Italian faltering as it is wont to do in public speaking, the audience rustling their programmes, and finally breaking into a relieved final applause. The book itself enjoyed a few weeks of glory in the bookshops and then disappeared with the rest of its kind into the far recesses of the gardening shelves.

Perhaps I was expecting too much; perhaps the world I am forever pursuing exists no more. Are book launches like this in England too, I wondered, going back home after this trying ordeal. I suppose they are, yet surely not those on horticulture. After all, as a race we adore our native plants and flowers; anybody who read Paul Scott's novel *The Jewel in the Crown* for instance or saw the televised version, will remember Rose Cottage up in the Indian hills where Mabel, the indominitable English lady who has spent her entire life in the subcontinent, ignores all the local flora in favour of her old fashioned tea and floribunda roses.

Now I know Palermo is not Simla, but why is it that here the English do nothing to promote their own flowers, refusing to plant lobelia, candytuft or any of that pretty white alyssum? Whatever happened to those wonderful rose bushes we had in our London garden – my mother used to get them free with toilet rolls I remember – great vermillion blooms which grew up to four feet tall; why aren't they here? Look at our gardens and balconies now and you'll find all the Mediterranean species growing. This is all the more serious as most English people just aren't used to watering sub-tropical bushes and flowers. Even the long-term expatriate who knows just how much water to give her flowers, and when, can occasionally overdo it. As Mildred once told me:

"One of the Mitford sisters gave her geraniums far too much to drink out in the south of France and my dear, they were all leaf and no bloom. One does have to be so terribly careful."

I think what we are trying to do out here is convince ourselves and any English visitors we may have, just how well and successfully we have fitted in to our foreign environment. We show them our riot of scarlet oleander, our luscious orange, lemon and fig trees, our magnificent jacarandas and creamy camelias and dare them to hold a lupin up to that. Yet underneath, we still long for the pastel hues of the herbaceous border, the snapdragon and delphinium, the wood-warmed summer house and lichened sundial.

Sissinghurst, where are you?

It is a different story I am glad to say, when it comes to our pets – dogs and cats especially. Here the English are definitely in the vanguard and will never allow their values to be undermined.

Most people will have heard about Rome's stray cats and how some eccentric old crone regularly goes out and feeds them. These animals may wander about the ruins of the *Foro Romano* and partake of the disgusting-looking plastic dishes of congealed pasta, but I'm quite sure they are neither sweet nor lovable. Mangey and with running eye sores, they probably leap away at your approach or hiss at the gently extended hand. Nothing at all like our lovely fat pussies back home.

Cats are definitely to be regarded with suspicion in Italy. Convinced – and rightly so – of getting a firm kick in the backside from anything Latin on two legs, they have, over generations, developed a deep-rooted mistrust of all human beings. Open warfare has naturally followed.

Some time ago I came face to face with the enemy while I was staying in a villa above Florence. It was early Spring I remember and still cold. Tuscany has a terrible climate with freezing winters and boiling summers and I can never understand why the English go on so about its wretched vineyards and stone farmhouses. I have lived in the neighbouring region of Umbria – which if anything has an even ghastlier climate with bitingly cold winds whistling through its medieval streets – and I'd never go back. One night in the villa, I was woken by a soft grating sound as though the cane chairs were being gently moved about the room. The window of our first-floor bedroom gave straight onto the tiled pitched roof of a small extension below. Beyond and all round that was the garden.

The noise made me extremely uneasy, as in spite of the cool nights, I remember having left the window open before we went to bed. Gently turning over, I reached for the switch and snapped the bedside light on. Aghast, I saw the bedroom was full of immense cats – poised on the dressing table, the tiled floor and even on the end of the bed. All of them froze, turning to stare at me, their huge eyes reflecting back the light. There must have been five or six of them: strapping ginger toms, swarthy blacks and ear-torn tabby toughs. Without thinking I clapped my hands several times very loudly and very suddenly, waking Franco up in terror beside me and sending the whole bevy of cats leaping three feet into the air. Flying across the room as one, they made a dive for the window, shot through and disappeared.

Now, you can't really imagine anything like that happening in England where cats purr and like to be stroked, and people are kind to them. But in spite of this difference, there's still no way the expatriate will be cruel to her pets. She may be regarded with amusement and incomprehension by the Sicilians, but she will not be moved. Her dogs and cats will be individually reared to eliminate any negative imprinting; regularly wormed, de-ticked, fed and exercised, and finally encouraged to look witheringly on their deprived conterparts.

I am not a doggy person myself and don't really understand the bonds that exist between people and their pets. I'll never forget the time at Golders Hill Park in Hampstead when I saw a gigantic Irish wolfhound coming towards me on a lead – it came up to its female owner's waist.

"What a wonderful dog!" I exclaimed, quite overcome.

To my amazement, instead of saying yes, it certainly was a magnificent breed and a very fine animal, the woman graciously inclined her head:

"Thank you" she said, and walked on. I might have been complimenting her on her hairstyle or her dress. Perhaps that is exactly how she did see her pet.

Dogs go through fashions in Italy and the fiercer or more unusual the breed, the better. English types are highly regarded, but so are the more exotic. So you get the husky and the chow chow panting away in the Sicilian heat and rubbing rumps with the perky little "west Eye-land wide" and the "cokk-air".

One of the unloveliest of all Italian breeds must be the Neapolitan mastiff, a huge, clumsy iron-grey animal with folds of flesh creased about a mournful countenance. Another is the stiff prancing little Sicilian hunting dog, a hairless sand-coloured animal with pink eyes and tight little testicles. I can put up with both of these as long as I'm not expected to pat or say nice things about them and as long as they are on a lead.

The brindled great dane in my local computer shop which pads around the shelves of floppy discs, likes to walk right up to the customers. The other day I saw him emerging from the back of the shop like an enormous black and white bridge with two six-inch lines of dribble slowly swinging from the corners of his mouth. I instinctively backed off.

"Don't worry Signora" the woman owner said "he's perfectly all right."

"I'm sure he is" I said, "but he's all dribbly."

"Yes" laughed the woman gaily "you're right there! None of us can wear anything smart any more, he ruins everything. That's why you see me dressed like this."

That was rich I thought; the proprietor and her family protecting themselves in overalls against this slavering animal and then leaving it free to muck up the customers' clothes.

6
Temptingly tranquil

Something rather strange has been happening this last decade or so in Britain – something so totally uncharacteristic of us and our way of thinking that it is worth taking at look at here.

Think of the old British Empire and the way it worked and you soon realise that one of its overriding characteristics was the imposition of our customs on foreign peoples. This went from the institution of the Anglican religion to cricket and the legal system, with a lot more in between. The rulers and the various missionaries would have seen it as doing what was best for the native peoples, but I wonder how often it occurred to them to ask themselves whether Indians or Africans actually wanted or liked the things we ourselves did. Perhaps not. Our way was best and that was that.

Back to the strange thing that has taken place in Britain: the way its natives have taken to the Italian way of life. People now kiss each other on both cheeks, Englishmen hug one another, we adore pasta and wine ,the Mediterranean diet is the best and healthiest in the world (those sun-dried tomatoes, dear), we think Pavarotti fabulous, we realise how beautiful the Umbrian hills are, we are even going over to Catholicism. How strange, how very strange... we *enjoy* foreign ways of life. Long after the Empire has ceased to exist, the English are now voluntarily accepting other peoples' customs. Nobody has *made* us embrace these things; we have come to the realisation all on our own. Nothing has been actively marketed by the Italians –

except the ordinary run of the mill travel literature – nor, I might add have the Italians themselves dreamt of adopting any of *our* customs, especially not cricket or Anglicanism. Unthinkable that the Florentine should choose to convert a farmhouse in Yorkshire for his Summer hols or that the Sicilian should go over to using lard instead of olive oil. And heaven forbid that their country should return to a monarchy – constitutional or otherwise.

How does the successful expatriate deal with all this? It's a tricky question. Back to the very early days and the kissing. Many years ago when I took Franco over to London to meet my family I was careful to warn him against displays of male affection.

"Now, don't on any account kiss my father when you meet him" I told him, "men don't in England."

"And another thing" I went on, "we only shake hands once – when we are introduced to someone. Never again after that."

The best thing of all was his kissing my mother's friends' hands. The rather admiring glances I had received as we drew up outside the London flat in our gorgeous two-seater sports car after having driven all the way from Palermo, were now doubled.

However, none of this meant that any English male friends would now start being chivalrous; it was still decidedly over the top and far too "continental"; practices you lumped together with the sharpness of Italian suits, gold chains and smarmed-downed hair. Besides, Englishmen had no idea how to kiss a woman's hand and would probably stuff it into their mouths or cover it in dribble.

Some years later it was still being considered just awful when footballers threw their arms round each other after scoring a goal. OK for Juventus and AC Milan of course, definitely off for Bolton Wanderers.

For a good many years I didn't consider the time was ripe for comment, yet I followed the gradual opening-up very closely from Italy. This opening had nothing to do with the EU but came simply from observing the obvious pleasure the Italians got from spontaneous physicality. The English conceded at last that it was all right to kiss your friends – actually it made you feel extremely Continental and less inhibited. So everyone began to do it.

The seasoned expatriate who realised how nice all this was ages ago but never had the chance of saying so, will now of course go round kissing everyone with great gusto and theatricality; the louder the smacks around the departure lounges of the various Italian airports, the more certain you can be of the long-established British presence.

"*Darling*! It's been simply wonderful. You just must come out more often. Enzo will be thrilled to see you, won't you Enzo? Now have you got those tomatoes packed safely?"

As far as food – and in particular pasta – goes, the change has been simply revolutionary. Not content with buying the commercially-produced stuff, the English progressed to the fresh home-made variety – something in fact the Italians themselves rarely eat. These were all shapes and sizes, tastefully displayed in rustic panniers in the tiny Hampstead and Chelsea shops which had nothing Italian about them at all. Englishwomen were now referring blithely to the excellence of their *gnocchi* and *pappardelle* instead of the corny old lasagne served up in pseudo Italian restaurant chains.

I remember eating a dish of this lasagna in a place in Euston. Swiftly microwaved, it arrived at table scalding hot with the blackened tomato sauce congealed on the sides of the oval dish and the cheese topping as tough as cowhide.

"Isn't it delicious?" my English companion said, tucking in. "Now don't tell me this isn't the real thing!"

Anyone who has been to Italy knows that the English overcook their pasta.

"They like it that way" an Italian restaurateur in London told me spreading his hands in resignation, "so I what can I do?"

In fact, Italians eat their pasta – whatever shape and whatever size – *al dente*, which means it still keeps its shape and doesn't collapse into a soggy heap onto the plate.

Fish too, in southern Italy at least, is firm and nearly always served up head, eyes, tail and all in the middle of a white china plate. The only concession to *haute cuisine* is the bit of lemon on the edge, but even this is plonked down in a thick utilitarian wedge rather than being sculptured into a delicate half-fan on the fish's back.

"How original" my English friend says surveying the fierce-eyed sea bass she is served up in Palermo.

"You said you wanted fish" I remind her, "this is *spigola* one of the best. That's the way we eat it here."

Note the "we" used by the expatriate to demonstrate the way her culinary tastes have moved on. Two quidsworth of skate, rock salmon and chips are very much things of the past now.

A lot of English people visiting Italy assume the expatriate knows about wine. She doesn't necessarily, although she will do all in her power to demonstrate the contrary. I was always flummoxed by it when I lived in England, but then of course hardly anybody drank the stuff and when they did, it was the man who was expected to choose. All we students could ever afford then was punch or Reisling and I never particularly liked it anyway. One had heard of Wincarnis or Sanatogen, but that was about all. Now, I find people are enormously impressed by my bringing out the names of two or three Italian wines when we are in a restaurant. No Sicilian would dream of describing his wine as being full-bodied or having a subtle bouquet, and neither would I. Besides, it is totally unnecessary; even the most humble of *vini locali* or house wines, will taste fabulous to the English palate. It's something to do with the heat and the scent of the Mediterranean and the good company.

Italian singers, like wines are often overrated or misunderstood by the English. Pavarotti for instance is the *Asti Spumanti* of *cantanti lirici* – which is not to say he isn't wonderful, he is – but rather that he is the one everybody has heard about. And that is the way he wants it to be. No rough brew produced in a small Sicilian cantina is going to make its name on the international circuit. Not yet anyway.

The successful expatriate likes Pavarotti well enough but tends towards the less flamboyant. The opera *Cavalleria Rusticana* is all right because it's about southern passions and therefore worthily ethnic (the noble savage and all that), but on the whole her tastes will be fringe-orientated.

But we were talking about how the British as a whole have decided they now like Italian music. What they really like more than the actual songs is the Latin image; would Pavarotti have made the big time I wonder, if he had been thin and not sweated. The handkerchief, gorgeous white teeth and massive frame all roar Italy! (but not Italia) to a quite deafening degree.

It is the same with holiday homes out here; in the sixties it was the Dordogne in France that was fashionable, now its the superbly restored farmhouse swimming pool sleeps four with stunning views over the olive groves in Tuscany. As I said earlier, I suffered agonies in the climate of this part of Italy as well as almost dying of exposure in a farmhouse there. But I was obviously unlucky; the majority of English seem to find such places enchanting. The other day in *The Lady* I saw an advertisement for a hotel on the south coast of England:

"Temptingly tranquil" (it read). "Relax, unwind.. quiet residents' bar.." and so on. The accompanying photograph showed an emerald green lawn stretching away to an azure sea beyond a pair of open french windows. The lawn had mown lines on it and there wasn't a resident in sight. Peace, quiet and old-fashioned hospitality featured very prominently. I saw in all the advertisements that hotels were small, private, secluded, and the sports reassuringly unaggressive and safe like golf, fishing and bowls.

This is a very far cry from holidays in Sicily. First of all as far as I know, there is no such magazine as *The Lady* in which genteel sojourns can appear and besides, tranquility is an unheard-of quality on any holiday here.

"I'm sorry Signora, but we have no call for peace and quiet in our hotel; our clients prefer a somewhat more boistrous stay. Perhaps the Signora should try the South Tyrol up near the Austrian border."

Perhaps I should. Yet one would have thought that on a small island off the north east coast of Sicily, peace and quiet would be easy enough to find – especially in May. And in a way I suppose it is.

Expatriates enjoy showing off these islands – the Aeolian Islands they are called – for apart from their lovely name, they are wild, volcanic, and almost uninhabited. English visitors love things like that and the Britishwoman abroad allows herself to share their enthusiasm. Harold had nothing remotely comparable to this after all.

A hydrofoil races you from the Sicilian mainland to the nearest island, Vulcano, in forty minutes. There are five other islands in the archipelago, all with enchanting names and all raising their heads lazily round about in the misty blue Mediterranean. Vulcano, pronounced Vool-*karn*-oh, is, not surprisingly, volcanic. This doesn't mean picturesquely like Mount Etna with little villages on its green-clad slopes, but fiercely bare, black and forbidding. It also stinks like a crate of bad eggs. This smell as soon as you land is overpowering, the sight of the ochre sulphur-stained rocks and coal-black sands quite horrifying. Bravely the expatriate tries to make amends,

"My goodness, this is fascinating! Just look up there at the steam coming out of the mountainside, have you ever seen anything like it?"

A small white van waits to take us to our hotel. On the way we pass a sunken pool near the shore; motionless human heads stick out of a softly bubbling cement-coloured liquid inside. "What fun!" I almost scream. (Perhaps everything will be all right after all.)

The smell has grown to unbearable proportions; masculine- looking women from Nordic countries stride from pool to sea in unlovely bathing dresses. It appears that the sulphur waters are good for you. If you can stand the stench. Handkerchiefs to our noses we leave our luggage in the white bungalows of the hotel and go out to explore. This really is a most extraordinary place with its tatty hotchpotch of souvenir shops and eating places strung out cheek-by-jowl along an unmade road. One of the many snack bars has a Sri Lankan pizza-maker standing morosely next to his brick oven in a deserted dining room, picking his nose. Barefoot men in necklaces wander up and down, dogs poke about in the rubbish tips.

Somehow we can't bring ourselves to get into the sulphur pool with the Germans; it all looks so unattractive and unclean. Instead, we have a light supper in the least depressing-looking of the restaurants. We drink a bottle of wine and don't notice night coming on. By the time we have paid our bill it is pitch-dark outside.

Everyone remembers the hotel is nearby, but in which direction it is impossible to tell. Thanks to the wine though, we set off in great spirits, arms happily linked. What a story this will make back home in England...

"There we were on this ghastly island, Mildred, in the pitch dark, without a clue which way to go. You should have seen us!"

Things ceased to be funny fairly quickly. Not only were there no lights at all, but there seemed to be no proper roads either. The extinct volcano with its jets of steam hovered eerily overhead and we could hear the quiet regular lapping of waves on the shore. Apart from that and the great arc of starry sky, there was nothing else at all.

"We ought to follow the smell" I said "I remember it's very strong right near the hotel."

We chose a path, set off and after five minutes ended up in front of a closed gate. We went back and tried again; it was getting frightening. There are no trees down there on the island so there was little risk of walking into one, but there were dips and craters to fall into and sheer slopes to disappear down forever.

In the end we found ourselves back at the restaurant and got someone to give us a lift to the hotel. It turned out to be at least half a kilometre away down a long very narrow path. We would never have found it. I was furious with the man at the reception desk.

"This is shocking" I began haughtily "there isn't a single light or sign at this hotel. How on earth do you expect guests to find their way back?"

He opened his mouth to answer.

"It's the most dangerous place I've ever been to" I went on incensed "we could have broken our legs or something. Why don't you light the place up?"

"We don't on Vulcano" he got in at last, smiling pityingly, "that's the way it's done here. In the summer you find your way back by the lights of the houses."

So tranquillity is indeed to be found here; all you have to do is to holiday out of season – any month that is except July or August – preferably on a small outlying island.

7
A brief visitor's guide to health matters

I came across the following guide in strange circumstances. Sitting one evening in the bar of Palermo's snobbiest and most grandiose hotel, I was trying to retrieve the olive from my scandalously expensive dry martini which had slipped down between the cushion and the arm of the very uncomfortable Empire style settee. Before my fingers closed on the cold oily little globe, they came up against a wad of papers. Drawing this out I found it to be six or seven pages of typescript full of crossings out and corrections, and now bearing a trajectile smear of grey-green olive flesh. After a summary glance I came to the conclusion that the guide had probably been compiled by a seasoned British expatriate or regular visitor to Italy – a considerably hardboiled and cynical one. Someone like Harold? No, no, far more like Mildred. Did she (for there was no doubt I soon saw, that the writer was a woman) intend it for publication, and if so, where? I didn't hand the manuscript in of course and I set it down here almost in its entirety. The only things I have left out are the little sketches the author had done to accompany some of the entries.

Discussions on and preoccupations with health, illnesses and medical treatment occupy an extremely important part in every Italian's daily life. The following is intended as an aid to tourists and prospective expatriates, but a more comprehensive study of Mediterranean customs is strongly recommended if readers wish to understand their hosts more fully.

Babies, overdressing of:
Apart from the hot Italian summers, babies are heavily muffled in fur-lined ski-suits for the rest of the year in case they catch cold. So swaddled are they, that all the English visitor is likely to see of local bambinos is a rigid pale blue or pink bundle being wheeled through the streets at great speed in a pushchair. The bundle frequently cries and tries to free itself from its Mr Michelin-like clothes, but is shut up by having a dummy rammed into its mouth and its fur bonnet pulled even more firmly over its ears. "He's getting cold!" is the terrified cry of the mother as she casts her eyes heaven-wards where one tiny cloud is floating across a perfect blue sky.

The author got the reputation of being a cruel and scandalous mother when she left her two babies barefoot in the pram on balmy Spring days. Cosy vests, flannel nightgowns, woolly socks and hefty little boots (see Scoliosis, fear of:) are standard Palermo babywear from November to June.

Bodily workings, fixation with:
One of the editorial breakthroughs of the century has undoubtedly been the weekly supplement on health matters brought out by a national newspaper. Do-it-yourself treatments have enjoyed the biggest success, followed closely by an A–Z of every known disease under the sun with cures and mortality rates. (I suppose you could compare this to our own British obsession with seed catalogues and gardening books). Sales of those newspapers offering the supplement have been further boosted by the "practical and elegant holder" provided on completion of the collection. If, after months of devoted readership, you have successfully reached this landmark, you may then be offered a custom built bookshelf on which to tastefully display (nothing about reading) your volumes. Italians are obsessed by the workings and dis-functions of their bodies – as a visit to any chemist will demonstrate. Here you will find the brilliantly excogitated storage system for the millions of medicines available: six-foot-long trays which slide silently outwards from a wall unit like corpse drawers in a mortuary. Take a look at the mind-boggling array of pharmaceuticals inside and compare it with the aspirin and cough mixtures in Britain.

I am considered antisocial in not suffering from digestive or liver troubles. (See Italians, common complaints of:)

Coffee, bloody nonsense about:
Italians are very rude about our coffee, saying they make the finest in the world. Theirs comes in minute cups which are only half full and drunk from in great discomfort standing up at the bar counter. "It's terribly bad for you" they say quaffing it down, "gives you heartburn". Coffee is so strong in Palermo that it brings the tears to your eyes, stains your teeth and makes your breath reek. Being the social equivalent of our cup of tea which gets offered to everybody at all times of the day, it's no wonder the Italians are highly-strung and over-stimulated. After attempting to be terribly Continental like them, the British resident invariably admits defeat and reverts to her cup of Twinings.

Draughts, horror of:
"You're in a draught" is one of the deadliest things that can be said to you in Italy. Draughts or "air currents" as they're known here, can cause all manner of dire consequences from influenza and joint pains to double pneumonia and death. There is very little difference in fact between cool breezes outdoors and draughts inside, and both are to be avoided at all costs. Ceiling fans too are frowned upon, and air conditioning considered absolutely fatal to health. In other words, anything that makes the Sicilian summer slightly more bearable is out.

Health Service, running of:
This is so painful a subject that I almost left it out. Having decided at the last moment to include it in my list, I feel bound to point out that no expatriate can ever hope to be successful in conquering, defeating or even peacefully coexisting with this disastrous and appalling system. Either she has to go private in everything or she must never get ill. One thing is certain: the middle classes are never seen in hospital beds or in public health-run surgeries. Never do they appear in noisy queues to have the referrals from the GPs endorsed by filthy-tempered clerks, and never do their white and anxious faces appear at windows to settle the charge or 'ticket' of their out-patient's visit. You may occasionally come across them in chemists, sneaking away with their stockpiles of antibiotics, but that is all. All the seasoned Englishwoman can hope to achieve in trying to preserve her status abroad is to make as little reference as possible to the rusty oxygen cylinders standing in hospital corridors, the washbasins with no plugs, the wards running out of

bed linen. The author however wishes to point out that in her experience, Sicilian physicians and surgeons are far nicer, kinder and more understanding than their English colleagues.

Hygiene, ambiguous attitude to:
Fruit and vegetables are so thoroughly washed in Italy that the housewife has to set a good ten minutes aside for the job every day. Some go even further and use lemon juice or soda to eliminate the dreaded germ. Incomprehensible to them how the English expatriate manages to consume the skin of the apple, and the jacket of the potato without dying. New clothes are washed or dry cleaned before use even if they came out of a sealed polythene bag in the shop, and houses are fanatically swept and polished. It is therefore odd how crumbs, old cigarette stubs, sweet papers and so on are happily chucked out of the window, and how many Italians will picnic on filthy beaches and put up with unspeakable public lavatories.

Italians, common complaints of:
Cervical arthrosis (whatever that is), liver malfunctions, anything to do with the stomach, all sorts of rheumatic aches and pains, slipped discs, acidity, constipation and everything digestive. The Italian is always one-up on you as regards complaints, and can cap any misfortune with a much worse one of his own. If your back aches, his is killing him; if you had slight indigestion in the night, he was rushed to Casualty with acute colitis, if you twisted your ankle, he broke both legs. Better to commiserate than to laugh. (Men far worse than women).

Smoking, battle with:
Sicilians still smoke quite a bit, particularly in hospitals, in front of the delicatessen counter of supermarkets and at petrol stations. The seasoned Englishwoman abroad is still horrified by this: "Do you realise we could all be blown sky high?" she tells the attendant filling the tank of her car. "Don't you bother yourself about that Signora" he smiles shifting the cigarette to the other side of his mouth and leaning even further over the tank, "no danger at all". My concern is considered extremely quaint and foreign.

Suppositories and injections, prescribing of:
The majority of English people knows neither how to insert a suppository or

give an injection. All Italians do. That is why doctors will nearly always prescribe one or other cure for common illnesses. "I can't give an injection" I used to say to the paediatrician or G.P. "Good heavens", came the reply, "well get your porter to do it then". And that is exactly what I did, (and still do). Up would come the rheumatic old concierge – man or woman – and give the husband, children or myself a jab in the buttock. When I asked how they learnt to perform such a delicate task, they said they watched their mother giving them, that anybody could do it and that they'd teach me if I wanted. I always declined. Suppositories are only marginally less dreadful to administer but at least they don't need a porter's help. I have no means of knowing whether we recovered more quickly than we would have done with English-type pills and linctuses, but the latter is undoubtedly less nasty.

Sweating, dangers of:

Children are forbidden to sweat. They have to run around, practice sports and play on the sweltering beach completly dry. One drop of moisture and that's it. "He's sweating!" is almost as dreadful a fate as standing in a draught, and if the two are combined, there's no hope at all.
Horror of perspiration is an interesting phenomenon and deserves further study.

Waters, taking the:

This continental practice, together with mud and steam baths has always been highly popular in the treatment and cure of various rheumatic pains and skin complaints. The fact that it is a complete con and achieves nothing at all is proved by the fact that Italians go back year after year to the same place. Sicily has tried more than once to jump on the bandwagon as regards spas and thermal stations, but has never been able to get her act together. It is easy to see why: famous watering places like Montecatini and San Pellegrino in northern Italy have an organisation and efficiency quite beyond the Sicilians' capacity. If you do venture into one of the very alarming natural steam caves on the island, it will be at your own risk. The 'doctor' is quite likely to go off for a coffee with his mates and leave you there for hours. Or the cold showers will have broken down or they will have run out of towels that day. The hot springs too which are also found here, are most unprofessional and uninviting: municipal-looking baths with no pampering nurses, pulleys or wheelchairs to get you in and out, just a snappy attendant who probably can't wait to get back to her telly.

In conclusion, the expatriate will probably go on sighing for the British National Health Service. No matter that many years have gone by and that things don't work there any more; she will stubbornly go on remembering the fatherly family doctor and the friendly and efficient hospital nurses. "Soon have you back right as rain, won't we dear?" Whenever possible she also preserves all those wise English pointers to good health; windows kept open at night (tormented by mosquitos), a brisk walk every day (exhausted by the heat), family picnics in the countryside (overrun by ants, no shade, no grass), and a winter swim before breakfast (freezing sea, voyeurs).

8
Dust is feminine

"Goodbye!" my student says cheerfully as he comes into the classroom and takes his seat.

"No, Salvatore, goodbye is when you leave someone, not when you see them."

"Ah, yes." he smiles and nods.

"You say hallo when you come in and...."

"Yes, yes I understand now."

"Under*stand*" I correct him, "not *under*stand. Put the stress on the second part of the word."

"Sì, sì." He lights up a cigarette.

"I'd rather you didn't smoke, the room's so small."

"Oh."

"Today" I tell them pushing an ashtray towards Salvatore, "we're going to look at the present perfect tense. Can anyone tell me the difference between I have spoken and I spoke?"

Nobody can.

I look at my watch: "it's ten thirty now: I have spoken English this morning, but I *spoke* French yesterday."

Silence.

"Is that clear? This morning is still continuing but yesterday is finished."

Here we go.

This has always been one of the trickiest rules to get over, and one which required a good deal of banging home. Nowadays it hardly matters at all; the Italian firms where I work want American English anyway and Americans as everyone knows, make no distinction between the tenses. I still have great difficulty in teaching "I just went to the rest room" instead of "I've just been to the lavatory". "Center" too, grates terribly, as does "traveler"; English spelling after all is so wonderfully illogical and was learnt under such duress as a child, that it seems cheating to take the easy way out.

Understandably enough, the Italian executives and computer researchers I teach couldn't care less whether a noun has two ells in it or one, but they do like a word to be as phonetically written as possible. My spelling has deteriorated badly over the years, making it increasingly embarrassing for me to answer their questions.

"How do you spell incongruous, please?"

"Now, I'm glad you asked that, Marcello. Does anybody know how to spell incongruous? No? Right: perhaps you'd look it up in the dictionary now and tell us all."

This is perfectly acceptable; my students are adults, courteous, and convinced of my validity as a *professoressa*.

Even my mistakes on the blackboard can be dealt with without too great a loss of face.

"Please, I not understand what the distbun is."

"Distbun?" I turn round and look at the board." Oh you mean *dust*bin!" I change the vowels around.

"Dustbin is where we put rubbish....garbage....The trash can."

Ignorance about British life – like my bad spelling and gallopping dyslexia – can be similarly circumvented. I have no idea how many members sit in the House of Commons for instance or what the order of rank of British peers is but I have to pretend that I do.

"Now, where's that excellent book I saw on the desk last week; the one with the lion playing cricket on the cover?"

"Over here."

"Good. Maria, I'd like you to look up how many members sit in the House of Commons, please. I must admit I'm quite surprised you don't know this, all of you; it's common knowledge." A sigh. "Ah well.... Right now, what does it say?"

Losing touch with one's country is an inevitable consequence of living abroad. Another is the rusting-up of the mother tongue. I must admit I never thought it would happen to me, and for a long time it didn't. But then came the first signs: the quaint turn of phrase I was apparently starting to use in letters back home, the wrong pronunciations, the thrashing about for the right word in conversation. After several years of this, "just a typing error" simply wouldn't do; it was all right and even rather endearing to be hopelessly out-of-date as far as British television programmes and personalities went, but rather shocking to have actually forgotten the Queen's English.

My literary translations make me blush with shame when I re-read them now, as do the various memories of my simultaneous translations. Alarmingly, as the years went by, I was finding it easier to translate from English into Italian rather than the other way round.

Fortunately for the interpreter, Italy is a land of congresses, meetings, conferences and seminars. No decision, however paltry, is ever taken without prior discussion, and the presence of the English interpreter (even though there may be no foreign speakers present) gives the whole thing tremendous prestige. Italians are very fond of talking, of mulling over all possible consequences, of seriously and profoundly "reflecting" before anything is acted upon. Venues too, as well as prominent speakers and "translating facilities", are of vital importance. The choice of a centre is an art in itself.

"That's not the right place at all for a congress" a seriously committed trade union leader told me sternly, referring to a well-known holiday complex on the island, "in summer the delegates look at the foreign girls on the beach and in winter they get bored."

Tut tut.

Despite this, a large number of conferences in Sicily – especially those held between June and September – are very well-attended indeed; not only by the participants themselves, but also by their families. Promises of wonderful seafood, strong, heady wine, sea bathing and sunshine bring them down in droves from dreary old Milan. I have worked at several of these; never as a simultaneous translator but as one who sits next to the speaker and paraphrases what has just been said. This is difficult in any circumstances and far more so if the subject and vocabulary are technical and unknown to you.

My worst experience (and I have had some terrible ones) was at a conference on infertility. So dreadful was it, that I still find it painful to write about. Like most locally arranged and organised meetings, the decision to bring in the translator was left to the very last moment. In this particular case, a translator was vital as the speakers were from Scandinavia and America.

I was sounded out:

"I can't do anything technical or medical" I said, "I'm not qualified. And besides, if the conference is tomorrow, I'll have no time to prepare anything."

"That won't be a problem," I was assured breezily, "first of all, it's not at all technical, and then you'll have a chance of talking to the speaker before the conference starts. She's a woman."

Infertility is a delicate subject and one in which the correct medical terms and vocabulary are absolutely essential; no professional interpreter would dream of taking on such an undertaking at so short notice and without adequate preparation. But this was Sicily, I was English, and as far as the Palermo recruiting agency was concerned, that was all that was required. I can only imagine that I was very short of money at the time, otherwise I cannot see how I could possibly have been persuaded to accept.

"Okay, I'll do it."

"Great. Tomorrow then, at nine a.m."

Although memories of the conference as a whole are hazy, I can still feel my frozen horror on hearing the Swedish speaker expounding at enormous length and with awful complexity on ova and Fallopian tubes, and of my forgetting everything she was saying. Words were literally floating away from me into thin air; I couldn't even understand what she was saying, let alone translate it into Italian. And to make things even worse, she suddenly broke off and swung away towards the blackboard:

"So: in this manner".

She sketched a few brisk strokes and dots with arrows radiating out from them, and there were grunts of agreement and approval from the body of the hall.

Finally she paused in her flow and turned towards me with an expectant smile. The conference hall was deathly quiet; there was absolutely no way I was going to be able to reproduce what I had heard. I opened my mouth and closed it again.

"Could you just repeat the last bit?" I hissed to her.

"The last bit?"

"About the..the...."

She did, but it was hopeless: everything came out jumbled and bungled. The very worst moment was when I translated spermatazoa as spermicide and the delegates exploded into incredulous and delighted laughter. Never have I felt so mortified and never so furious with myself for being there in the first place. My own fault entirely for being so unprofessional.

Translation in medical conferences is arbitary anyway, as everyone knows what is being talked about, and can quite well dispense with the services of an incompetent Englishwoman up on the platform. And this I feel can serve as an excellent example of what the successful expatriate definitely should not attempt, unless that is, she happens to be a professionally-trained interpreter. But in that case, she probably wouldn't be an expatriate anyway.

I once tried to give myself proper standing by applying for membership of one of the professional bodies of Interpreters and Translators (northern-based of course), but gave up the idea almost immediately on discovering that a hefty sum of money was the only requisite. Skill and experience seemed quite by the way. And you couldn't have that, could you?

No, the Englishwoman in Palermo should aim for a far vaguer and more mysterious status: a Prominent Member of the British Community will do quite nicely for instance, or – if she is slightly more ambitious – The Woman who knows all About Plants and Gardening. If she wants the cash and prestige without the hard work, she might try for the English Lecturer Everybody Has Heard About at the University, thus securing for herself all the best translating work in town. I am generally known as The One Who Writes:

"Oh, Gay writes, didn't you know?"

"No."

"Well she does. Books and things."

"Are they any good?"

"Well, I ...."

There is absolutely no need to elucidate on one's activity: the less definable it is the better. "Gay writes" after all, is decidedly preferable to "I don't know what Gay does." Reputations abroad are more easily built up and consolidated by the skillful use of vague references to one's talent.

What worries me about talent is my growing inability to employ it properly. It is bad enough losing familiarity with my own language, without having difficulty with Italian. It is the genders: English speakers just cannot get into their heads – which words should be feminine and which masculine and what it is that governs that logic. I have heard foreign correspondents in

Rome, British-based writers and HM consuls all making the same errors.

There are only two nouns that I can think of in the English language that we give feminine status to: a ship and Britain, and only one human being – a baby – that is neuter. All the rest are conveniently it or he and she. In Italian, on the other hand, you have to know that dust is feminine (why?) and book is masculine and that all accompanying adjectives conform to that premise. "The dust is thick on that piano" is perfectly acceptable in English, but "the dust (feminine) is thick (masculine) on the piano" sounds dreadful to an Italian.

A common practice for English people in Italy is to let their sentences die away or to get a fit of coughing before they finish speaking so they don't have to put the correct endings onto the words:

"I wonder if you'd mind passing me that pile of green textboo....."

"I'd like three hundred grammes of that mild, blue chee...."

Our accent anyway is thought rather comical and endearing. Frequently parodied with all the stresses misplaced and an atrocious pronunciation, it is the voice of Laurel and Hardy in all their old films. No longer is there another fine mess to get out of, but *un vero pasticcio* (oon vair-oh-pas-*teech*-oh). Hardy has become Olio, Laurel, Stanlio.

Writing as well as speaking, is not easy. I once gave a short story to my publisher here. He phoned me some weeks later:

"It's absolutely full of grammatical mistakes" he said "quite unreadable". This was dreadfully humiliating for someone who'd been in the country so long. When I first came out, I remember, the patient Sicilians would communicate with me – as they do with all foreigners – in infinitives, making it easier for me to understand:

"You to go to the language school at five o'clock, to do your teaching there and then round about nine, I to pick you up and we to go to eat. Do you to understand?"

You can't imagine the English doing that with foreigners. If you don't understand the lingo mate, bloody hard luck.

"It's because we're a multi-racial society" I tell miserable Italians who have visited Britain and not been able to find their way about," there are so many foreign people around; we don't mean to be rude".

Why not tell them the truth and say Londoners really couldn't care less whether effing Salvatore and Carmela get to Madame Tussauds or not?

Of course, you're not always treated with courtesy here, even if your are

English. I was given rough treatment some years ago at a conference on Immigrant Women from the Third World. My only claim to being a speaker there was that I was English and had written a book about my experiences in Sicily. It was to be in Catania which is over two hours drive from Palermo on the other side of the island, and I was to take a pile of the recently published book to try and sell at the same time.

The first thing that went wrong was that during lunch in a *trattoria*, a crown fell off one of my teeth; I had to go upstairs to a disgusting ill-lit lavatory which had no mirror and nowhere to put a handbag, to try and fix it. It was such a small room that you had to flatten yourself against the washbasin in order to shut the door and anyway the bolt was so bent that it couldn't be shot home.

It is quite amazing to me how comparatively smart restaurants in Italy can have such terrible toilet facilities and how customers are willing to put up with them. Usually, like this one, they are right at the top of a flight of steps or down in the basement, or even worse (and surely illegally) bang next door to the kitchen so you have to ease your way past clashing crockery, steaming vats of pasta and an hysterical chef.

Once I had fixed my tooth and finished lunch, I had to find the conference centre. It turned out to be a huge hall with a sea of empty chairs, the first three rows of which began to fill up with agonising slowness. I was put up on the platform with an M.P., a social worker, a leading member of a women's organisation and a young Ethiopian woman who never stopped smiling throughout the entire proceedings. Introduced as a writer and author of the book "available at the back of the hall" (I never sold a single copy), I was to speak on the foreign woman's work experience in Sicily.

This I duly did only to be attacked later on by the grossly fat women's organisation leader who accused me of having it easy:

"We can hardly compare Gay *Marks*' experience with that of immigrant Filipino women in Sicily" she began, "she's been lucky and hasn't had to struggle. She is one of the priviledged."

I have never thought I was similar to immigrant Filipinos, and I am sure they have no wish to be anything like me – we are quite different. And if I was priviledged as the old cow claimed, then I certainly wouldn't be sitting here in a draughty hall in Catania. I told her all this afterwards, but it was plain she didn't like me or what I represented.

I didn't find this meeting at all funny at the time, although looking back,

I can see it does have its comic side. Humour is of course subjective and people laugh at quite different things as I discovered years ago at the cinema.

The Hampstead Everyman cinema in London has always shown what it considers "quality" foreign films – mostly French or Italian of the neorealism school. Good old standbys I particularly remember were De Sica's *Bicycle Thieves*, Fellini's *Cabiria* and Truffaut's *Les 400 Coups*, although the Russians and Japanese got a look-in too.

Always shown in the original with English sub-titles, these films were projected in the Everyman's claustrophic interior before a mixed Continental and English audience. The absence of trailers, cartoons and newsreel (always part of the the much jollier and unpretentious Odeon and Regal programmes) and the severe black and white in which these masterpieces were made, left one in no doubt whatsoever as regards the management's intellectual commitment. Screenings in fact were nearly always watched in reverent silence. Except that is, for the laughs. The audiences were mixed because Hampstead used to have a shifting population of different nationalities – and perhaps still does. They seemed to be mostly Italians, Spanish, French and Greek Cypriots then, and in fact some of London's first foreign restaurants and coffee bars grew up along Heath Street and the High Street.

Anyway, during a French film for instance, the audience would suddenly burst out laughing – the French contingent that is – leaving us English staring blankly at a sub title such as "you awful man, I'll make you pay for that", which wasn't funny at all. Something else must have been said to set them off because girls would even give the occasional shocked and delighted scream at the altercations between swarthy toughs of the Parisian underworld, so obviously we were missing something.

When I came to Italy and began understanding the language, I realised a bit to my surprise that it was the swear words that got some cinema audiences going. Admittedly we were watching the brightly coloured "social comedies" or Spaghetti westerns the Italians made so brilliantly, and not some gloomy old post-war misery. Still, it did seem odd.

Why for instance should "fuck-off!" make you *laugh*? Well, it seemed to. Another thing I noticed that got them rolling in the aisles were the fights; not the vicious stuff you get now but the sanitized and highly aural knockabout of *A Fistful of Dollars* or the banging of heads together and chucking out of the window of the Italian-style *Bonnie and Clyde* imitations.

Benny Hill, still hopping over Italian television screens, is considered faintly smileable – a typical product of British humour. But situations and people we consider wildy funny often leave Italians cold. I once showed part of a Rowan Atkinson video to some adults studying English. Maybe it wasn't all that funny, but I thought it was. It had hardly any dialogue so it wasn't so much for the language but more for the questions English teachers have to put to their students:

"Now Carmelo, where was Mr Bean sitting in the first part of the clip? Was he alone? What was he wearing? Did anyone notice why he had put on gloves?"

I realised something was wrong almost at once as not only was nobody laughing, but one or two had even begun looking at their watches or out of the classroom window. This was the sketch in which Atkinson consults a rare medieval book in a reading room library and manages to spill white eraser liquid all over the illuminated script. Appalled at what he has done and terrified of the consequences, he tries to cover up the damage by tearing out the page.

One or two of the students managed a polite smile but I could see they thought I was exceedingly odd to want to show such a thing. Yet here was the cowering, put-upon, self-conscious male, the epitome of English repression; surely they'd find that amusing. They didn't.

Oddly enough, there is an Italian equivalent of Mr Bean; he's called Fantozzi, pronounced Fan-*tot*-sy, and is the humble clerk in the government office who is constantly put upon. The character was created by a comedian called Paolo Villaggio (or Paul Village). Fantozzi has been going a very long time and in fact his creator is now an overweight, wild-haired and raddled old pro who has greatly enhanced his failing funniness by being known as the last actor to work with Fellini.

One of the most brilliant Fantozzi sketches goes back to the beginning when the series was shown on television (he later went onto film) and shows him being received by his office boss into the holy of holies. The suave and sleek-haired *dottore* seated on a sort of dais commands Fantozzi in ringing tones to enter and take a seat. This is an oversized leather bean bag on which the miserable Fantozzi try as he will, cannot get a purchase. From his elevated position the boss watches him writhing and pushing the bag into shape with undisguised impatience:

"Take a seat I said, man. Take a seat!"

"Yes at once sir, I'm just trying to get my..."
"Will you come on! I haven't got all day!"

Finally managing to fit his backside into a depression in the seat, Fantozzi prepares to listen. But even as he sits there, the bean bag slowly and inexorably begins to sag backwards, tipping its miserable incumbent further and further backwards until he is lying, supine, his head resting on the floor, his heels towards the ceiling. And still the boss, oblivious and by now well into his stride, continues to deliver his diatribe.

It is a wonderful bit of comedy, yet I remember being the only person who laughed till I cried; everyone else found it only mildly amusing. Now this could be because I saw my Englishness in it or because the Italians themselves do not find the put-upon particularly funny. Villaggio went on to develop the character until he became a grotesque parody and *that*, strangely enough, was when he really took off. And when I lost interest.

What was interesting to me was the discovery firstly, that the underdog does in fact exist in Italy's extrovert society, and secondly, that he is not considered a particularly humorous character. On the contrary, here it's side-splitting to be one-up on the next man, a spiv, a con-man, and the more deviously successful you are at it, the better.

9
A play, a parcel and some sardines

Anyone who hasn't been to Italy, again according to Dr. Johnson, will always feel inferior, as there are things in that country he should have seen and has not. It's easy to see how this belief came about, at least in the eighteenth century. Those after all were the years of the Grand Tour when gentlemen of means and scholarly bent took to the Continent in search of culture and refinement. Although they rarely found the latter, they professed to be suitably impressed by the former. So impressed were they in fact that they packed up and carted off the best of Greek and Roman sculpture and took it back home to enjoy at their leisure in their vast and obscenely overstuffed English residences.

Culture and Italy have remained indivisible over the years; there is a sort of aura about the very word "Rome" for instance, as though its inhabitants still strode about in togas and behaved themselves in a wickedly decadent manner at table (which to a certain extent they still do). Florence too has a decidedly unbalancing effect on some British minds, appearing as a delightfully dreamlike Renaissance world, full of medieval jousting horsemen.

Sicily does not come up by a long chalk to the efficiency of the capital or to some of Italy's other regions in marketing its cultural heritage. The island's particular fame rests on its mysterious Greek, Arab and Norman influences with a nice fat helping of baroque thrown in. Feeble attempts are occasionally made to plug this unfashionable historical hotchpotch but such efforts are invariably thwarted by yawning, nonchalant neglect leading to the inevitable decay of its monuments. Finding and visiting such antiquities thus becomes quite an undertaking.

The Sicilian homeless for instance, can frequently be found ensconced in the crumbling wings of eighteenth century patrician villas or in deconsecrated churches with their washing lines strung between priceless statues and once imposing staircases. These families who tend to have snarling dogs straining at the ends of pieces of rope, exude an intimidating air of proprietorship which is very off-putting to visitors. You feel as though you are trespassing on their domain instead of walking about a national monument.

"Excuse me, I'm so sorry, but could you just move your saucepan from the altar? I'd just like to get a closer look."

As these families' privacy is usually guaranteed by telling you the building is "under restoration" and "too dangerous" to visit and as the authorities rarely seem to intervene or care, a whole series of Arab mosques, Norman castles and baroque churches are slowly and inexorably sinking beneath the ground.

The successful expatriate shows a healthy interest in all things cultural. This helps to build her reputation as a connoisseur of Italian art among visiting countrymen and women.

"One can hardly imagine the situation reversed" she laughs gaily pointing to the chickens pecking in the Cathedral close in Cefalù, "squatters shacking up in Fountains Abbey – I mean how frightful."

How I envy Harold Acton gathering the cultivated of Europe about him in his villa! That voice with its turn-of-the-century English: "orf" for off, "moo-earning" for mourning. A voice that went with knee-length tennis frocks and topiary. Somerset Maugham, Waugh... how they would have smiled and reminisced, leaning back in basket chairs on the terrace enjoying their cocktails and the view of Florence in the gathering dusk. And nearby, hovering respectfully in the background, would be the devoted Giovanni:

"*La cena è servita Eccellenza.*"

"Splendid. Are we all ready gentlemen?"

A creaking of wickerwork chairs as famous bums are raised.

"What's it to be tonight Harold? Oysters, or whatever you call'em out here?"

"Wait and see Evelyn; I've got Maria very well-trained, and I can promise you a first-class dinner."

Over the candlelit meal the elevated talk would continue, snatches of poetry would be recited by heart, fine wine savoured.

You just can't do that in Sicily, and not just because time has moved on. The climate's right after all, the wine's as good, the vegetation and the light are as lovely. It's just that, well, people consider the island too *foreign* and too far away. Gentlemen on the Grand Tour rarely ventured beyond Naples; a few intrepid women did, but they were usually rather mannish and far more likely to be interested in Sicilian weeds and butterflies than culture. Had these British made the extra effort and crossed the Straits of Messina, they would I think, have been awe-struck by what they found waiting for them there – the vast Greek amphitheatres of Syracuse and Taormina for instance, where the tragedies of Sophocles and Aeschylus are played out.

Like going up Mount Etna, Greek theatres are one of the things foreigners Have To Do in Sicily. A lot of Sicilians would never dream of doing either of course – especially not going to sit in a draughty old amphitheatre.

"Well, if you really want to" Franco says one August evening.

"Yes I do."

"Well, what are they doing, *Medea, Antigone*?"

"No, it's a modern play and it's in Gibellina."

The small town of Gibellina up in the hills in the Belice region about an hour's drive from Palermo, was totally destroyed by an earthquake. On the fifteenth of January 1968, a hundred and eighty-five people lost their lives crushed under rubble or swallowed up into chasms in the roads. The survivors were rehoused (many years later) some miles off, and the abandoned ruins left just as they were. You can still drive through them: silent, collapsed heaps of stone, slate and rafters frozen in mid-slide on the hillsides. It's a chilling experience. An open-air theatre was then built here as a sort of memorial – more of a simple stage really with an open space for seating. I had always wanted to go.

The Sicilian summer season is marked by theatrical and musical events: modern plays, light opera, Greek tragedy and concerts, all performed outdoors. A bit like the London circuit I suppose, Glydebourne, the Open Air Theatre in Regent's Park, the Aldburgh Festival and so on. Except of course that here in summer it never rains.

Attending these events tends to be a bit upper-class, that is, more of an evening out than a love of culture. Palermo audiences frequently chat through concerts or quite openly wave to their friends on the other side of the tiered arenas, "*Ciao carissimo!*" and get quite offended it you tell them to be quiet. These are people who have either not left the city during the torrid months of July and August and are bored stiff, or others who are equally bored in their seaside and mountain retreats and have come for a breath of cool evening air. What's going on up on the stage is relatively unimportant. This particular play – a new work about a nineteenth-century peasant uprising had been reviewed very well and I was looking forward to it.

We had terrible trouble finding the theatre; dusk comes down very swiftly in Sicily, and we had missed the exit on the motorway. By the time we had located the first signpost to the Ruins of Gibellina on the twisting country road, the outlines of the hills were melting into a violet sky.

"What time does it start?" Franco wanted to know.

"Eight-thirty" I said, "we'll never make it." I am obsessed by punctuality even though it has no relevance whatsoever to Sicilian life.

"Yes, we will."

"Are you sure the theatre is in the ruins and not the new town?"

"Quite sure."

The road wound on and on, growing narrower and dustier. This couldn't be right I thought looking at the miles of empty countryside all around. There were no trees, just the occasional agave plant with its single tall fibrous stem rising straight up unto the sky. A large bird of prey wheeled overhead and I saw the first star come out.

Then an old cream-coloured Fiat *seicento* came bowling along the road towards us raising a cloud of dust. We flagged it down.

"Excuse me, could you tell me if the theatre is this way?"

"Straight on." The driver, a *contadino* with fierce black stubble and a flat cap leant right out of his window and jerked his thumb into the hills behind him, "keep going." And he disappeared in a choking cloud of dust.

I couldn't imagine any kind of civilisation being at the end of a road like this. The ground fell away on our right and rose steeply, now chalky and spotted with tussocks of coarse grass to the left. Then coming out of a bend, the road sloped suddenly downwards and we found ourselves in what looked like the bottom of a stone quarry. Cars were parked at odd angles all around and a well dressed crowd was picking its way carefully over boulders and rubble-strewn ground.

"This must be it" I said.

No theatre in sight, just rocks and white dust. There weren't even any lights. Everyone seemed to be walking up a slope in twos and threes so we parked the car and followed them and very soon came to a makeshift workmens' hut with a tall, bespectacled youth completely filling it. It had a single lightbulb hanging from the eaves. This was evidently the box office.

"Has the play begun?" I asked him breathlessly

"No, not until ten" he said "How many tickets?"

"But it said eight-thirty in the paper." Will I never learn?

The youth took no notice: "through there when it's time" he said handing over the tickets and indicating a large wooden gate sagging on its hinges. A rusty iron chain bound it to its post. It looked like the entrance to a building site.

It was quite dark now. And we still had an hour's wait. I smelt roasting aubergines and sausages. And there, on top of a sort of shelf wedged into the quarry walls, was a long, low booth brilliantly lit and emitting clouds of smoke.

At that monent an elegantly-dressed woman came slithering and screaming down the loose shale towards us, a glass in one hand and a hot dog in the other.

"Help! Darling!"

She reached the bottom at our feet. High above, next to the food stall, an athletic white-haired man in jeans with a maroon cashmere pullover knotted casually round his shoulders leant over:

"You all right Vittoria? Hang on, I'm coming down."

"Let's go and see what they've got to eat" I said, after taking this in. We clambered up.

The smart and totally unsuitably-dressed public were occupying a collection of ghastly old tables and rickety wooden chairs laid out round the stall, eating, drinking, and making a great deal of calling to each other in loud voices. So packed was it that we could hardly get to the counter. Inside the stall, food was being dispensed by a hatchet-faced couple – quite obviously locals and on to a very good thing indeed. Keep going Giuseppe and make the most of it, it won't last for ever. Husband and wife in fact were going flat out, grilling slices of aubergine, *panelle* (small flat cakes of chickpea flour), chips and sausages, all at breakneck speed, flinging them inside rolls, and shoving them over the counter accompanied by paper cups of rough white wine. All at exhorbitant prices. Sweat streamed from their faces, thousands of lire disappeared into their apron pockets.

Nearby, the immaculately white-suited mayor was holding court, making quite sure his reputation as a "character" did not go unnoticed by wearing a overlarge wide-brimmed panama. He kissed my hand when we were introduced and carried on talking:

"I can assure you, this'll be an unforgettable evening; marvellous acting, and extraordinarily perceptive writing." He paused to take a quick look about him, then went on in a louder voice to the group gathered around him: "and don't miss the African dance group we've got next Friday – they're quite remarkable."

I turned away:

"Gay! *Carissima!*"

It was Titti, a ferociously fashionable friend dressed tonight in tight black pants, very high heels and huge gold hooped earrings. "Got thousands of friends to see and then off to the prince's for the weekend. Can't stop! Bye!"

The play itself was almost totally incomprehensible to me being in broad Sicilian dialect, but it didn't matter at all as the setting was so magnificent. There was no stage as such, just the gently convex hilltop on which the actors formed shapes and dissolved, telling the story of a peasant uprising against Sicilian landowners that went disastrously wrong. As the moon climbed higher in the sky and little fires were lit all over the hills, the spotlights roamed beyond the stage, picking out other actors in the distance and a group of men, women and children who came slowly singing over the brow of the hill towards us.

* * *

The entry phone buzzer went:

"Yes?"

It was the postman: "Magazines and newspapers for you, Signora."

I thanked him. Our letter boxes are set into the wall in the entrance lobby of our block, but these can only take letters; the bigger stuff, parcels, voluminous junk mail and so on, has to be put somewhere else. The rolled-up *Independent on Sunday* supplements I get from England are regularly left in the plant trough, so when I come home I have to thrust my arm deep into the fronds of the Kentia palm to see if anything's come. Nobody except me seems to think it the least bit odd that parcels should be left like this; so far, my Sunday supplements haven't been watered together with the palm, but it'll probably happen one day. Or somebody might like the look of them and take them away.

The postman is a tiny grey-haired man who gets to our block at about half past ten in the morning. If he's ill or off work we don't get any post at all. Two, sometimes three, dead days can go by like this, then everything will arrive together. This is obviously the fault of some crazy disorganisation up at the post office, not his at all. He's a cheerful, talkative man and when a long-awaited letter comes I feel like asking him whether he's over his 'flu now.

The huge modern post office which co-ordinates postal deliveries in our area has just introduced a barmy system for dealing with the public. As it is taken for granted that Sicilians don't queue, new ideas are always coming up to corral them into some sort of order. This latest one means that before we can go up to one of the windows, we have to get a ticket from a red machine in the post office entrance hall. First a button has to be pressed to select the window needed (parcels, stamps, pensions, payments or whatever) then, at the sound of an electronic ping, the desired counter can be approached.

The other day, my ticket for sending a large packet was numbered 4003 but there was nobody else before me. Despite the furious pinging all around I was seen-to straight away. I don't know what happened to the other four thousand and two customers. Things went quite differently however the day I had to collect an even larger package from one of the counters. The package contained video and audio tapes as well as several large books, and had been too bulky for the postman to deliver. A card had been left telling me to pick it up here. Once again, my name was spelt wrongly. Although I've been called most things in Palermo, "Gas Mask" I have to admit, was certainly the most original scrambling of my name.

"What's this?" the girl behind the glass-fronted desk said turning the card over.

"I have to collect a parcel" said Gas Mask, "look, it says so."

"Mm. Well I can't give it to you now."

"You have to. It says I can collect it between 9 am and 12 midday."

"The colleague who deals with this is off today."

"Listen," I said "I've come all this way and I want it now. This is the right counter and the right time; please let me have my parcel."

"I can't..."

"I WANT IT NOW!"

She scuttled away and came back cradling my parcel.

This furious asserting of my rights goes very much against my nature and I could never have imagined myself shouting in public in the old days. Before I came to Italy, that is. Now, on the contrary, I feel a quiet, inner satisfaction, and don't take at all kindly to being downtrodden. Self-esteem is important I tell myself. Raised voices in public places in Palermo are viewed by others as normal, often inevitable, occurrences anyway. But what kind of reaction would there be if I started roaring away in the quiet orderly queue of the Building Society in say, West Hampstead?

"She must be Italian, dear, and Italians are so volatile, we all know that."

"Yes, but what's she going on about?"

"Shh! Don't shout.... I really don't know; something about her account I think."

"Dear, dear, foreigners are so excitable, aren't they?"

Actually, the last time I *was* in the Building Society I found myself all tensed up trying to defend my place in the queue. It's a reflex action; I always forget that you don't have to bother in Britain, that it is quite unnecessary and that nobody is going to push in front of you.

* * *

One of the most agonising decisions the successful expatriate has to make is whether to corroborate foreigners' views of Italy. When she is consulted, does she confirm their already-formed theories; does she agree with them on the chaotic disorganisation of Italian cities and split her sides laughing – as they do – at the antics of their hosts? Does she sigh and shake her head at the corruption of Italian politics and the tenacity of the Mafia? Dear, dear, dear.

This after all is what visiting journalists are in Sicily for – to have their ideas confirmed – so why not give them what they want? Their brief is to do a story on the Mafia or the Mafia victims, or the family of the Mafia victims, and that's what they are going to do.

"A bit of gore, Mike. Not too much. A couple of interviews with someone who's stood up to Mafia threats (or if he's been murdered, with his widow); an enlightened politician, some Jesuit priest if he's about, an aggressive feminist – you know the sort of thing. You've only got fifteen minutes air time so for Chrissake make it snappy. Hire a car and get up to

Corleone too if you can, and speak to Riina's wife.... Oh, and try and get hold of that Englishwoman – Gay something-or-other – some kind of journalist or writer; apparently she's been out there for God knows how long. Probably quite round the bend by now, but give her a call anyway."

I am quite sure Harold Acton was never put through any of this; his questions would have been on Etruscan vases, Benvenuto Cellini and the Cinquecento.

"Tell me Sir Harold, how would you define the influence of the Renaissance on present-day Italian society? And would you agree with me, I wonder, that Michelangelo's early work has much in common with Tiepolo's blue period?"

"Right, Gay; first of all, perhaps you can fill me in a bit on that murder last Wednesday out at the sewage farm. Were there fifty-three or fifty-four bullet holes in the body?"

If I want to preserve my status as Someone They can Talk To, I have to keep fairly closely to accepted views of a corrupt, violent and chaotic Sicily. If on the other hand I presume to dissent and say it really isn't that way at all you know, I will very quickly lose that status. I have already had words put into my mouth (and into my pen) that I never said or wrote. The mental set certain journalists bring with them means they are deaf to anything they don't want to hear. And there is nothing we can do about that at all, is there?

Giving an off-the-cuff opinion can be difficult for me anyway as I am not naturally eloquent either in Italian or English and need to prepare my answers beforehand. Even arguments of a far less serious nature than crime can present problems.

As in the case of the coffee ice cream.

A lot of people will have come up against the Italians' sense of local pride – *campanilismo* as it is called. The word comes from the *campanile* or bell tower found in every village square. In saying my bell tower is higher, better, more beautiful, more efficient etc. than yours, you are demonstrating your superiority over neighbouring villages and people. In these fraught and difficult times it is more a question of my village/town/city is less awful than yours, has fewer burglaries, car thefts and so on.

It never occurred to me before I came to live in Italy to be proud of West Hampstead – even if it had had a bell tower. I knew that northerners in Britain were meant to be very attached to their cities but I couldn't really understand why. There used to be a catchphrase on a radio comedy programme I remember, which had the studio audience in stitches. "If you 'aven't been to Birmingham" this Brummie character called Marlene went, "you 'aven't lived." Laugh laugh laugh, deary-deary me. Wipe the tears of mirth away. I think it was Birmingham and Marlene, but it might have been Manchester and someone else.

Anyway, a good deal of Italian local pride concerns food: there are recipes and specialities for instance that only they have and only they can make. Our almonds are better in this village so our biscuits are naturally superior to anything else you'll ever taste in Sicily, and certainly in mainland Italy. Never will you eat an almond biscuit like this Signora, never. And I'll stake my life on that.

These fierce convictions can get embarrassing for the outsider especially when she is required to put the victual to the test. After attending a meeting in a small town in the province of Enna recently, Franco and I were taken to a café to taste "our famous coffee ice cream." It was half past eight in the evening and I didn't want ice cream.

"Now I want to know what you think of this Signora" I was told as an arm guided me gently towards the gleaming glass-fronted counter. The ten or twelve oblong stainless steel containers inside were filled to the brim with creamy maroon, rich ochre, cool apple-green, fudge-like beige, chocolatey brown, and sparkling white confections.

"Just look Signora, eh?.... What do you think of that!"

"Lovely, but I don't think I'll......"

"Totò! One of our special cornets for the Signora – you won't get anything like this in Palermo, I can assure you!"

Oh dear. "Well only a small one, thank you."

But Totò piles two huge scoops of the soft pale cream onto the very slender cornet, making a big thing of winding, folding and pressing. It'll take me ages to get rid of that.

"Thank you. Oh, wonderful!"

Eyes are fixed on me. I take a ladylike lick. Must think of something to say.... something technical perhaps about the texture or flavour...

"Well?"

"Delicious! The coffee is....really...so..so.. coffee-like."

"There! What did I tell you? It's an exclusive recipe; all made by hand with real coffee. None of your artificial essence here, no Ma'am."

Thank God I'd said the right thing; in relief, I branched out and got quite daring:

"And it's not too sweet either. Some are so sickly, aren't they?"

"Exactly!"

"The sugar is in just the right proportions: not too much or too little." I was going from strength to strength.

Here's somebody who knows what she's talking about:she may be a foreigner but she certainly knows her ice cream when she tastes it. Good for you Signora.

The truth of the matter was, it was pleasant enough but I had tasted just as good elsewhere. Wild horses wouldn't drag that out of me of course, and anyway all this was valuable grist to the expatriate's mill. Here was a way I could extol the virtues of Real Italian Ice Cream first-hand. Never mind that we were only allowed Walls and Lyons when we were kids, and that Joseph's Genuine Neapolitan Ice Cream van was definitely off limits (we've no idea what he puts into the stuff, dear). Things have changed.

"Of course" I tell my visitors, "you know the finest ice cream you can get is in..." (I give the name of the town). "It's made exclusively with real coffee.The real article mind you, none of your ersatz essence stuff."

Some days later I took the same English friends to one of my favourite restaurants up in the mountains: a tiny *trattoria* with superb local cooking run by two partners. So impressed were my friends by the food and drink that after the meal they asked the cooking partner over to our table so they could compliment him. Unfortunately he was off that day so we had the waiter partner instead.

Perhaps it was because he had been standing-in for the absent cook or perhaps it was the warmth of our praise that did it, but he got completely carried away. The pork we had so enjoyed was no less than sucking pig, the ricotta had been rushed to our table straight from the sheep and so on; I almost expected him to stagger in with the wretched ewe to prove his point. When we got onto the wine, he surpassed himself.

"The grapes in that wine were pressed by the peasants' feet, you know."

Now that was really going too far, even for Sicily. Peasants simply don't climb into wine presses any more. Misunderstanding our incredulous faces, he made it even worse:

"But of course they take their boots off first!"

Well, it was our own fault I suppose and only to be expected; one should never show oneself quite so overtly delighted with everything, or quite so readily impressed – it's just asking for trouble. Especially in Italy. A bit like politics in a way.

"I suppose you vote in Italy?" people often ask me. Well yes, I do; in fact I must have spent a sizeable chunk of my life inside Italian polling booths. To be eligible to vote in England, I'd have to be resident in the country for several months at a stretch, something which so far I have never done.

To my shame I must admit that I have never been wholly convinced of my choice of Italian candidates. It's a case of conflicting images again. Look at that chap standing for the forthcoming provincial elections on the poster over there – the one with a surname like a strangled shout: "Eye-*ell*-oh!." Now, I might easily be swayed by the lovely coloured backdrop of the bay of Mondello behind him mightn't I, and not bother about his proposals or track record at all? The choice of this nearby seaside resort on his poster clearly indicates he is standing for our constituency – as though we were all illiterate and could only connect by pictures. Does the local candidate for London N.W.6 have himself photographed against West End Lane Fire Station, I wonder. If he does, the Palermo contestant might well be expected to get the most votes, after all, sea and palm trees are far prettier than fire stations.

While she has grave reservations about expressing opinions to the British press and media, the Englishwoman abroad is perfectly willing – nay, anxious – to show friends how absurd the whole business of Italian politics and politicians is and how comically flummoxed she is by it.

"I mean really, you've simply no idea.... how can one be expected to choose between all these parties/groups/factions/candidates? It's so much easier for you in Britain with only two parties."

"Well yes, I suppose it must be."

"And all the referendums we have too: yes or no to hunting, divorce, the return of the House of Savoy, recycling our rubbish..." (I was getting carried away), "it's just impossible."

"Mm. I can see how confusing it must be." A pause: "but aren't you used to it all by now?"

The trouble is, I am not, not really, that's the strange thing. The British Expatriate in the Algarve or Tossa del Toro, the one who has hasn't gone and married a foreigner or perhaps renounced her citizenship, can go on casting her vote in the UK. So of course can the serious upmarket settler like Harold. But the dye is cast as far as I am concerned.

"Well dear I did tell you: you can go wherever you like but you'll never find a place like England. It's the best country in the world."

If you say so Mildred.

I most emphatically do.

* * *

On summer evenings village women and girls like to sit outside their front doors in a little semicircle of dining room chairs crocheting, preparing vegetables or just chatting together. They face inwards, not out towards the road. Elderly men on the other hand always sit in a long line – again on the same uncomfortable wooden chairs – but this time facing outwards. They prefer the village square or outside the social club and are inordinately fascinated by everything and everyone that passes by.

Village houses tend to be very cramped with a steep flight of stone steps immediately inside the front door leading up to the first floor. The houses give straight onto the pavement which is usually very narrow and which the housewife considers as her own property. She'll sluice it down and put gera-

niums and ferns outside which she grows in old olive oil or tomato paste tins.

By looking at the walls of their houses instead of the street I think the women are demonstrating their modesty in the same way that they will cover the lower part of their balcony railings with canvas so (I am told) men cannot look up and see their legs.

All this as you can imagine is most peculiar to the English way of thinking; I'd never have thought of men looking up at balconies in the first place. When I first came out and was given a lift on an Englishman's vespa, I was told (by the Englishman himself) that I had better ride side-saddle as that was the way women did it in Palermo. As we sped through the old streets of the city I felt rather as though I should be dressed in a long black hunting dress and veiled hat and be giving the rear mudguard a touch of the whip. It goes without saying that I have never sat in a semicircle outside my front door facing inwards and never intend to do so. I certainly didn't at Concetta's house.

I met Concetta in hospital in Palermo a couple of years ago where we were both to have eye operations. She came from a little fishing village about thirty kilometres out of Palermo and only spoke Sicilian dialect. She never could get hold of my name properly but then neither could the male nurse:

"Which one of you signoras is.." he said coming into the ward and consulting his clipboard, "...Guy Mar-kess?"

"That's me" I said.

"No breakfast. Operation tomorrow morning."

So I was Guy Markess to the hospital staff and something like "Kane" to Concetta.

Hospitals are run along quite different lines to their English counterparts. Here, for instance, relatives can visit any time they want and with no limit on number. Our little ward was frequently bursting with sons, daughters, husbands, aunts and uncles. Friends too. All talking very loudly together and at the same time.

They nearly all belonged to Concetta and were absolutely fascinated by me. She had obviously filled them in about my extraordinary accent and mysterious country of origin. Our beds were next to each other so I got the full force of their friendly curiosity. Concetta's husband was tiny and always came dressed in a suit and flat cap. He was a fisherman and travelled daily into Palermo to see his wife by train and bus. It took him several hours and as he had already done a night's fishing and was no longer a young man, used to arrive looking exhausted.

Concetta was muscular and terribly fierce-looking but with a sweet nature. It was she who straightened my bed and helped me wash when I couldn't get up. Nurses of course are meant to do these things but are usually quite happy to let relatives or more mobile patients get on with the job. Poor Concetta could hardly see, so when she brought the basin of water to my bed, she managed to soak the sheets in the process.

She was also a voracious eater and polished off her hospital meals faster than anyone else – and mine too when I couldn't manage them. If her husband had had a good catch the night before, she would be brought some fish dish wrapped in brown paper and would eat that too together with an entire loaf of freshly-baked bread.

It is considered courteous in Sicily to offer some titbit from your meal to anyone nearby who is not eating. You even see grown men in cafes in Palermo sharing their coffee. So it was that I had *sarde al beccafico* – stuffed sardines – pressed on me one afternoon by Concetta's husband. This is a very rich and highly flavoured speciality consisting of fresh sardines rolled up and stuffed with a mixture of garlic, breadcrumbs, pine nuts, parsley and currants and then fried in a great deal of olive oil. The conconction was so oily in fact that it had left large dark grease stains on the flimsy paper in which it was wrapped. There was no question of refusing.

"Delicious" I said suffering a good deal.

After we were discharged from hospital, Concetta and I kept in touch by phone. I always knew it was her because she shouted at the top of her voice down the line and asked to speak to Kane. One afternoon we said we'd come and see her. Her village is near enough Palermo to have become a popular seaside resort; people have built or rented holiday homes along the coast and in the foothills of the surrounding mountains. It is still picturesque – at least out of season – with its cascades of purple bourganvillea, narrow streets and cobalt blue sea.

Concetta and her husband live in a very modest little house right on the quay; when you open their sitting room window and look out, you see the fishing smacks pulled up right underneath and swathes of nets spread out over the cobbles. It's an looked enchanting sight. But neither husband nor wife can get to sleep in summer for the shouting and blaring music of holidaymakers which goes on till two in the morning.

They seem sadly fatalistic about this state of affairs believing they are quite impotent to do anything about it. And they are probably right. But as both were born and brought up in the village and have lived in the same house since they were married, it must be hard.

True to type, Concetta keeps the bit of pavement outside her front door swept and washed. It's all done with great energy and banging of brooms and pails which drives her husband and grown-up children mad with anxiety.

"I don't want to rest and I can't just sit and do nothing" Concetta wailed as she served us ice cream in their kitchen, "I always have to be doing something. It's the way I am."

She would have made a wonderful nurse with her tremendous energy and urge to help others, but women of her generation and background were never expected to have a job of any sort outside that of mother and homemaker. Now probably in her early sixties, she is frustrated by her forced inactivity and poor eyesight. Concetta would never dream of sitting facing the walls of her house crocheting with the other women.

10
Palermo

This is a good place perhaps to say something a bit more about my relationship with Palermo. The area I live in was originally a *borgata* of the city. A *borgata* in Sicily is not a village or even a suburb as we'd understand them in England, but something rather more amorphous. There is nothing remotely picturesque or charming about *borgatas*; they are usually just a collection of gimcrack flat-roofed houses which locals have put up on the outskirts of large towns or cities.

Most Italian cities have them; Rome's *borgatas* for instance are notoriously rough and dangerous and have always held an irresistible appeal for certain film makers and writers. The homosexual Pier Paolo Pasolini who used to roam them at night in search of fiercely beautiful boys – both for his films and for himself – was found murdered there one night crushed under the wheels of a car.

As far as I can see, there was no town planning whatsoever in my *borgata*, and roads just appeared where they'd be useful to whoever had built himself a house there; that's why they wind apparently aimlessly and dustily in and out of the surviving orange and lemon groves or come bang up against a stone wall. Drainage was primitive and smelly, and still is.

The *borgata* nevertheless tries to be like a real village or *paese* with a tree-shaded square where men can play bowls and have a game of cards, and an adjacent bar where they can hand in their pools coupons on Saturday nights. Shops were originally little more than holes in the wall housing bakeries and rather horrific butchers.

The area has not escaped the property developers – I live in one of their modern blocks right under the sheer wall of Monte Pellegrino. This blissfully wild and deserted mountain is dotted with irregular clumps of sturdy little firs; large-horned cows graze on its lower slopes in autumn and spring, and there are buzzards and (they say) chameleons too if you care to look for them. From the top of Monte Pellegrino you can look out across a shimmering stretch of Tyrrhenian Sea to the island of Ustica and overland in the opposite direction, past the green Madonia mountains to Mount Etna.

Below my flat are half a dozen or so of the *borgata's* surviving houses strung out in an irregular but defiant line between the modern blocks and diminishing patches of countryside. As the fortunes of these original inhabitants go up and down, so do the exteriors of their dwellings. The man who trundles plastic bowls and household cleaners round the streets on his van has just added another storey to his house, so he must be doing well. *And* he has enclosed his patio with a high whitewashed wall.

This cantakerous but long-suffering *borgataro* goes out every morning about half past seven, easing his creaking van out of the garage with much grumbling and coughing. Only a strip of windscreen is visible under the overhang of blue and orange plastic buckets, lavatory brushes, and detergents strapped to its frame. His missus is obese and hysterical and much given to bawling to some unseen relative behind closed shutters.

When serious and – one assumes – legalised, building began to get underway in our *borgata* some of the more enterprising of the original inhabitants cashed in on the new amenities provided for our posh new flats by stringing wires from roadside telephone poles to their own houses. *Fili volanti* or flying flexes these are called, and you can see them looped in great swags all along the outsides of the old houses.

The same thing I imagine went on with the drainage systems with little channels running from back-street houses to unseen central collecting tanks. It is all a question of equal opportunity: if the facility exists then one is licensed to make use of it. It's every man for himself in the chaos of Palermo's *borgatas*. Either that or you go under.

I am known as the *Signora Inglese* round here and as such, someone for whom allowances have to be made. The other day I asked a new greengrocer who had suddenly appeared at the roadside if he had any kiwi fruits. The request was idiotic, kiwis in the borgata are like prickly pears in Bognor.

"No" he said pityingly.

"Well what about these" I said nodding at some huge yellow globes.

"They're peaches" he said very slowly and clearly.

"I'm very well aware they're peaches" I told him, "I just want to know whether they're juicy or not."

* * *

Survival of the fittest in such a rapidly expanding city as Palermo has naturally put paid to a lot of the old districts. To create a good impression when the city hosted the World Cup in 1990, a massive new square was built opposite the football stadium. This replaced a filthy but fascinating jumble of tenements, stalls and taverns. Goats I remember, used to wander onto bits of waste ground there, and the traffic always snarled up as it tried to get past the fishmongers' stalls which overflowed out into the road.

Then one day the area was cordoned off and the whole thing demolished. It was like a battlefield afterwards. One old man who sold fried *panelle* and potato croquettes on the corner, refused to leave his stall. They told him he'd get blown up with everything else if he didn't, but he wouldn't budge. Finally, they called him away, pretending he was wanted urgently, and as he hurried off, someone pushed his vat of oil over, laughing as the liquid spread out over the road. He had to be forcibly held back as his pathetic little stall was bulldozed. I found this a very sad story.

The new square, Piazza De Gasperi, was never completed in time for the World Cup, being left as a no-man's land right up until last year when its centrepiece was furnished with four palm trees and a piece of sculpture on a plinth like a pile of dog excrement. According to the authorities, the sculpture had been donated to the City of Palermo by a Korean of some standing and could not be removed despite public protest. It is still there.

Not far from here another area was demolished. Half a block of flats disintegrated in a few seconds in Via D'Amelio – blown up by the bomb that killed judge Borsellino and his police guards in July 1991. Someone I know left her appartment there in a daze after the blast to find the lobby and entrance of the building gone and the road full of glass, twisted car carcasses and bodies. Human limbs were hanging from the branches of the trees and there was blood everywhere.

She tried to stop her small son from seeing the horror everywhere before collapsing semi-unconscious onto the kerb. When the police arrived, they wouldn't let her or any of the other residents back into their flats. She has never got over the experience psychologically and I don't suppose she ever will.

* * *

There's a sophisticated side to Palermo – downtown Palermo as some of the guidebooks call it. You instinctively know everything's going to be wildly expensive there by the shininess of the glass in the shop windows on its main thoroughfare, via Ruggero Settimo. It's not a long street and at its first intersection, goes dramatically downmarket, with fat unfashionable families and hostile-looking North Africans jostling each other on its crowded pavements. If you stand still at the leather goods shop at the traffic lights, you can literally have one foot in the posh part and the other in the seedy one.

I often wonder whether the smart set do an about-turn the moment they reach the traffic lights as you never see them beyond this point.

"Right Silvana, you've got your shoes and silk underwear at last, and I'm completely whacked. Now can we please go back for an aperitivo at Roney's?"

Roney's is a fearfully smart café, definitely worthy of Harold Acton, where you sip tiny drinks behind a slightly burnished plate-glass window. The whole point of going there is to be seen, and the right way to do this is to sit back in your cane chair and stare disdainfully about you. It's a very Italian activity.

Roney's however wouldn't have been a patch on the famous Bar Romeres owned by Franco's great-uncle and *his* father before that. An institution in Palermo from about 1860 right up until the late 1940s, the Bar Romeres was bang in the fashionable heart of the city at the *Quattro Canti* crossroads. People of fifty-plus still remember Isidoro, the eccentric waiter who used to listen in on the conversations of the cafè's aristocratic customers, and write them all up in the gossip column of a local paper.

Beyond and behind the muckier end of Via Ruggero Settimo and stretching down to the sea, lies the original Palermo: a glorious hotchpotch of baroque churches, ornate palazzi, statues, fountains, squares, convents, monasteries and markets, all scandalously being left to subside and crumble away into oblivion. This is where the Sicilian counts and princes resided when they were in town. Not many still do, for it costs a fortune nowadays to make these great houses habitable, and the aristocracy don't have fortunes any more.

I was quite excited when I was introduced to my first Sicilian prince, but he turned out to be extremely ordinary: small, grey-haired and tired – not even romantically decadent. I don't really know what I was expecting.

An untitled but distinguished lawyer I once interviewed for a magazine article who still manages to survive in his magnificent old palazzo, proudly showed me what he had done to halt decay there. He now had central heating and a lift and there wasn't a peeling cherub or chipped caryatid in sight.The mansion itself is wedged halfway up a filthy alleyway – the sort of place you feel decidedly uneasy walking along.

"I always tell people who come here for the first time not to bring a handbag or any money with them" the untitled lawyer said comfortably as we leant on the balcony railings looking out onto the bursting sacks of rubbish below. "Mind you, they know me here, and I have no trouble whatsoever" ("they" obviously being the muggers and petty thieves swarming here after dark).

Why is it that the robbers, highwaymen and bandits of Sicily's past are so romantic while modern-day thugs are so lacking in glamour? If you say to an English person that you were set upon by bandits in the Sicilian mountains, it sounds thrilling:

"Really? What did they *do* to you?"
But if you tell them your handbag was snatched by two youths on a motor scooter in a Palermo market, they'll say it's disgusting and the delinquents should be locked away for good.

Sicilians for their part, have this thing about our own homegrown villians; people like Jack the Ripper operating in the gloomy backstreets of a permanently fog-wreathed and mysterious London. I was asked by my publishers here why on earth I didn't write a novel set in the 19th century, instead of the other stuff I was bringing along which really wasn't saleable.

"You know, murderers, hansom cabs rattling over the cobbles, unspeakable maimings and disfigurements – nice and gothic."

"Yes, well....."

"Plenty of fog – or "smog." You get fog all the time in London, don't you?"

"No. Not after they brought in a law against burning coal. There's smokeless fuel now."

This always comes as a great disappointment.

I don't write about the Mafia either, although I've been asked to. Much nicer doing little pieces on Palermo and its inhabitants. I used to have a weekly column in a paper – a diary kept by a fictitious and unwordly Englishman I'd called Professor J. Fitton-Smythe who was permanently baffled by everything he came across in the city. The cartoonist on the paper had done a lovely sketch of him which appeared above the article. He said he'd based the physical features on Harold Macmillan and there was certainly a definite likeness.

One of the things which struck Fitton-Smythe (and me) was the way the smart and the seedy co-exist here. My very expensive dentist for instance has an immaculate waiting room with glossy yachting magazines spread on low glass tables. He uses the latest equipment and techniques and has nurses clad from head to foot in spotless white who quietly soothe your fears. Yet the brass plaque outside the door is tarnished to a dull black and is coming unscrewed. Millions of lire for a crowned tooth and his name is illegible. Oh dear.

Very occasionally I hold a course of English at what is known as a cultural centre. Several of the students are from foreign universities who have come to study Italian in Palermo, others, like the ones I teach are executives from companies who need English for their work. You'd imagine a reasonably clean and tidy place, wouldn't you?

It was during a boiling hot spell at the end of last summer when I went into the classroom and threw open the windows to get a bit of fresh air. I couldn't believe it – outside on the balcony like some awful nightmare, was a gigantic jasmine with branches as thick as walking sticks, arching high over the wrought-iron railings and poking into the crevices of the masonry. Thousands of shrivelled brown flowers carpeted the floor like the carapaces of dead cockcroaches. I called the secretary in and pointed to the botanical monster:

"Time that was cut down a little," I said gaily, "or we won't be able to get out onto the balcony any more!"

"Oh I rather like it" she said, "still, I suppose it could be trimmed back a bit."

Nothing was ever done and I had to give my lessons with the dreadful plant leering in at me at the window. I longed to take a pair of shears to it myself, but knew this would be taken as an insult. None of my students paid the slightest attention to the jasmine. I expect it's taken over the whole building by now.

11
From Decorators to Manna

Our flat needed re-decorating.

"We'll have it white again" I said, because white is the right colour for the Mediterranean and pictures look good on a plain background. Ten years' tenure had left its mark; the kitchen ceiling had very dark corners where grease and steam had accumulated. When I pointed this out to the man who came to give us an estimate, he said:

"My word, yes, it certainly is in need of a clean." He glanced out at the balcony, "but why don't you glass-in your balcony and put the hob and oven out there?"

This isn't as strange as it sounds; a lot of people living in small modern flats do it. You gain an extra strip of floor space it's true, but have to sacrifice your balcony. A balcony for me means plants and sitting outside all the year round.

"I've glassed in *my* balcony" he went on "and my wife does all the cooking out there. So now we use the kitchen as a sitting room. And you should see how clean my ceiling is!"

It was clear he valued clean ceilings very highly indeed.

"No" I said, "we'll keep things as they are."

The decorators moved in the following week; there were two of them – the *mastro* or gaffer and his assistant.

I fell immediately in love with the mastro. He was tiny with a very round head and lovely rolling walk and I liked the way he made a special effort to speak proper Italian to me. Although I understand Sicilian perfectly well after all these years, I wouldn't have dreamt of using it with him – neither would he with me – it would have been quite the wrong thing to do. Men speak Sicilian very easily and naturally amongst themselves and across the social classes but don't usually include women in this intimacy. And certainly, a foreman wasn't going to speak it to a foreign signora like me.

Actually there wasn't an awful lot of dialogue going on between the *mastro* and his mate. I realised the mate wasn't very bright nor as thorough as he should have been. I could tell this by the terse way the *mastro* ordered him to clean up the distemper spills from the floor.

They were terribly quick and efficient – no tea-breaks or anything like that. At about noon they'd down tools and tell me they were off for lunch. After barely three quarters of an hour they were back at at work again. They had started in the kitchen by swathing everything in huge polythene sheets. It was only the ceiling to be done there as the walls are tiled, so that was soon over. When they moved into the sitting room where my piano and computer are I got nervous.

"Do be careful about moving the piano won't you?" I said to the *mastro*.

"*Non si preoccupi, signora*. Don't you worry" he said with a lovely smile.

"And the computer. It's very delicate."

"*Non si preoccupi, signora*."

I listened out for sounds of my new Japanese piano being hauled roughly over the ceramic floor and then took a look round the door jamb (they'd taken the doors off) to see how they were getting on. The piano was in the middle of the room and the mastro already painting the ceiling. He wore a boat-shaped hat made out of newspaper, had a cigarette stuck in the corner of his mouth, and was wielding a roller on the end of a long pole.

"My computer...?" I began

"*Non si preoccupi, signora*."

I got him to leave all the nails in the walls so I'd be able to hang the pictures up again in the same places, but then noticed that they'd rusted with the water-based distemper, and got him to take them all out. Then I was worried they'd leave gaping holes.

"*Non si preoccupi, signora*."

I stopped worrying and in three and a half days the flat was finished –

cleanly and beautifully – inside and out. I wondered whether things were as efficiently carried out in Britain.

* * *

There was a torrential downpour soon after the decorators left, and with the rain came the prickly pears. These gorgeous fruits appear at the end of the summer like swollen thumbs on the thorny pads of the huge *opuntia ficus indica* cactus. This hideous but prodigious plant tends to form lethal barriers in the countryside which are quite impossible to penetrate.

The best way to eat prickly pears is chilled and peeled and the best place, one of the street stalls. My favourite one stands outside a crumbling ruin of a building which, so the plaque says, goes back to 1690. Apparently it was a shelter for "poor virgins at risk," but whether "poor" referred to their economic situation or to a lapse in sexual behaviour I don't know.

Prickly pear stalls are unique to Palermo; there are only two surviving ones I know of although they must have been very common at one time. This one has a sloping counter covered by a perfect arrangement of pears, all just touching each other like graded eggs in a box – one sort at 4,000 lire a kilo, the other (plumper and bigger) at 5,000. Behind is the garishly painted landscape of a dangerously smouldering Mount Etna and four cactus plants on a dry featureless plain. In front of this depressing scene the owner has placed a tiny Sicilian cart complete with mule and mulateer wearing the traditional Sicilian costume of black, white and red. Fairy lights wink around the cart's painted flanks. One of these – "Alfio kills Turiddu" – shows two stiff-limbed and very clean peasants locked in combat, with the taller of the two holding a knife. This is instantly recognisable as a scene from Mascagni's *Cavalleria Rusticana* and has nothing whatsoever to do with prickly pears. An oval portrait of Palermo's patron saint, Santa Rosalia, again surrounded by fairy lights, completes the decor.

The owner sits next to a battered old fridge watching the passing traffic. When he sees us coming he very slowly gets to his feet and lifts the cover of the fridge as if it were a great effort. Notoriously morose, prickly pear men never greet you or ask what you want.

"Four" in fact is all Franco says. The man dons a pair of very thick rubber gloves, lifts four pears out of the fridge, weighs them on a pair of brass scales and takes a large knife. Holding one of the pears in the palm of his left hand, he tops and tails it, makes one vertical incision, another around its middle and swiftly peels off the rough skin.

He holds a puce coloured fruit out to me in his gloved hand; it is cold and deliciously sweet. The next to be peeled is Franco's; crimson lake this time and dripping with juice.

As we eat, the man stands patiently by with the next peeled one ready in his glove. As Sicilians eat very quickly, prickly pear consumption is like an assembly line: eat one, ready for the next, eat the second, in with the third. And so on. Genteel English ladies don't eat like that at all, and I am making very slow progress. I keep glancing worriedly towards my second pear gleaming in the rubber glove; it is a brilliant orange this time. I shove in the last dripping morsel and hold out my hand for it.

You can eat lots of funny things in Sicily; down the road from me for instance is a man who sells snails and bunches of dandelion leaves. The snails are always crawling out of their basket and I hope some of them at least make it to safety. I could never eat a snail – especially not one plucked with an awful suck off the rim of a basket on the roadside, but then I know many Sicilians couldn't bring themselves to eat an English sausage.

I have tried over the years to introduce the family to nice English food: bread and butter pudding, potatoes in their jackets and so on, but have never had much success.

"They're so delicious" I used to say about baked beans in a tin, "just try. You don't have to eat them all, just one or two."

I know too they dread Christmas because I still insist on traditional English fayre and they don't want to hurt my feelings by refusing.

Everything about childhood is so different out here. Italian schools for instance are nothing like ours; no familiar grammar or comprehensives like I remember, no GCEs or GCSEs. No proper headmistresses or headmasters. Children go from elementary and middle school to what is called a *liceo*, a fearfully high-powered course of study where teaching methods are based on the practice of *interrogazione*, an oral dissertation on the previous lesson or lessons. A student selected at random has to stand up in class and talk on some aspect of what he has – or should have – studied. That's probably why Italians are so much more articulate than we are.

There are no school uniforms and text books are not provided. What is more, the Ministry of Education makes quite sure texts are changed every year so that parents have to fork out again and again every September. Even if the texts are the same from one year to the next, the editions change, so you can't win. We must have spent millions of lire over the years to furnish our children with books.

One of the horrors for me of those schooldays were the parent-teacher meetings one had to attend. We would be summoned once a term to hear the teachers' assessment of the child. I loathed and dreaded it. It's the custom here for parents to help their children with their daily homework, when they are small by making sure they actually get down to doing it, and when they are in secondary school, no less than by lending a hand.

This was impossible in my case; Italian teaching methods were totally foreign to me, and anyway I had no knowledge of mathematics, Latin, history, philosophy, Italian grammar or literature. I had never read Dante or any other of the Italian poets. All the subjects I thought I was proficient in like art, English literature and music were totally useless out here.

The only time I remember helping was when my daughter was in primary school and had to learn a tune to play on the recorder. I knew the musical notes by letters: middle C, D, E and so on, but in Italian the notes are known by the tonic sol-fa. So middle C in Italian is do, D is re, and so on. I just couldn't handle it.

"Right now, let's begin: now wait a minute...fa...fa. That must be G..no F... Hang on."

The recorder was flung against the wall and I was never asked again.

When parent-teacher day came round I had to be suitably dressed and at the school by four o'clock. It would already be milling with formally dressed mothers in a hyperactive state about their children. All of them knew what subjects their children were weakest in and in which they had excelled.

No attempt was ever made by the school to organise things properly – each parent being called in alphabetical order for instance to talk to the teachers – nothing like that. It was simply first come first served, or rather, the nearest to the classroom door got in first. So we waited for admission, pressed against the door in a heaving mass. This would then open a crack, and the school caretaker's face appear:

"Next."

Someone would squeeze in, then the door would be shut again. If you were right at the back of the scrum, you could still expect to be in school at seven in the evening.

Inside, the teachers sat hatchet-faced all round the edge of the room, each with his or her register on the desk in front of them. Parents began on the right of the door, slowly working their way round and taking the flak as it came.

"Now Signora, I'm afraid your son has not been doing at all well in geography this term. Not at all well. I don't know what has happened. Has he any personal problems at home? Either that, or.... I mean just look at these marks."

A nasty horny fingernail ran down the list in the open register, stopping at our surname.

"Look at this Signora, I mean, you can see for yourself...six. five...<u>two</u>. Now what are we going to do, mm?"

The dreadful unanswerable question was addressed directly to me.

My Italian just wasn't up to it:

"I know, yes, I am realising... perhaps he isn't been well that day. He really must try harder, I do realise that."

Although I had been told beforehand by my distraught children, I never remembered who was who on the staff.

"Now, don't forget mum, the history teacher's the one with the bun and glasses and the hairy mole on her chin. Don't forget. She's the *professoressa* Lo Piccolo. *Don't* go saying I was at the beach the day I was meant to be *interrogata*; say I was ill. Okay? Mummy do you understand? And try to speak proper Italian. Please."

Very occasionally the teacher was nice and non-aggressive – usually the young priest taking religious instruction.

"But what exactly do you *do* in R.I?" I once asked my son. "Nothing," he replied, "some of us just go off or wander around, or else he talks about quite different things."

"What things", I wanted to know, "Drugs? Sexual problems? Jesus?"

"No of course not."

In spite of the tension of these meetings and the stress the children are under during their schooldays, I noticed they nearly always had an affectionate relationship with their teachers – something I never had with mine.

Carnival was another trying time. Celebrated every year in February, it is one of the unavoidable occasions on which mothers have to be actively involved. It's the fault of the schools again; kindergartens insist on keeping a special day during Carnival when all the little ones traditionally turn up in fancy dress.

They look sweet – tiny policemen, Robin Hoods, Japanese geishas, Marie Antoinettes and so on. But the outfits are terribly elaborate and wildly expensive. I felt it morally wrong to spend vast sums of money on something ready-to-wear when the whole point of dressing-up is to do it yourself. That's the fun, and that's the way we always used to do it as children. The old dressing-up box and all that. Here, they were all so unimaginative with their ruffles and frills and everything just so. I wasn't going to be bludgeoned into doing it the Sicilian way.

As Carnival came round each year I was regularly asked for a bought costume – a puce crinoline perhaps or the Mexican bandit Zorro's black and gold outfit (complete with sword.)

"No. I'll make it" I said, "it'll be far more fun, you'll see."

My favourite standby was a clown because I could swathe my children in cast-offs and old dusters. And what fun with those red noses and huge smiling mouths! I still have the official photograph from the kindergarten showing the whole school sitting on the garden steps dressed in gorgeous and expensive costumes and elaborate head-dresses – an explosion of purple and gold bandannas and turbans, doublets and hose and bewigged 18th century gentlefolk. One small down-mouthed clown sits amongst them in patched trousers and a false nose.

My greatest triumph should have been the Indian costume I made for my daughter one year. I used a swathe of real orange silk for the sari, worn over a black swimming costume, going around the waist and gracefully up over one shoulder. She had gold sandals, bangles and a proper red dot on the forehead.

February can be very warm here, and my daughter was now in a progressive and boisterous junior school. The red dot on the forehead vanished almost immediately and much worse, the sari gave way with a rending fart of silk in the playground, unravelling itself into a train of frayed orange across the gravel. The Indian lady had to be pinned back into her costume, and I was never allowed to forget it.

"When in Rome.." should have been branded onto my forehead long ago; perhaps then I might have made a better mother.

* * *

The tight control exercised by Sicilian parents over their female children produces obedient and unadventurous daughters. They are also articulate, presentable, clean and courteous.

Mmm..

Looking back over my own upbringing in which I was never threatened, punished or forbidden to go anywhere or do anything, I have to admit I had none of these qualities except I hope, the last two. Obedience was neither expected nor given in our family; it was simply a question of mutual respect. I wasn't even really presentable until I came to Italy and learnt how to dress properly.

As a parent I simply brought up my children the same way. I couldn't have done it any differently. While I never came up against criticism or hostility, there were surprised (and maybe even scandalized) reactions which reached me via the kids.

"You're so lucky" friends apparently told my daughter – not because she came from a rich or famous family, but because she had an English mother who allowed generous freedom of movement. They liked coming round to us in the afternoon because there was English Cake and you put milk in your tea.

Food is important to children everywhere but Italy (and perhaps France) must be the only country where it is held in such reverence by adults as well. Mealtimes for instance are sacred here. The first thing anyone asks on telephoning between one and two pm is:

"You weren't at table were you?"

If you say well yes, actually we were, the friend will immediately offer to ring back later. This respect for mealtimes can partly be explained by the fact that it's a social occasion with the whole family sitting down together, something that's perhaps quite rare in Britain now.

There's a completely different attitude to food here; Sicilians after all were munching their way healthily through the Mediterranean diet while we were still on rock cakes and smoked haddock. And it wasn't just a question of climate or poverty; England was just as poor after the war. I do remember eating some wonderful things though – blackberries and raspberries, for instance – although I never tasted manna.

Manna is the sweet gum of the flowering ash tree, and manna production used to be quite an important cottage industry in the town of Castelbuono up in the Madonie mountains. The gum, obtained from the bark of the tree and collected in a dish, was used in the manufacture of sweets and laxatives.

In the early 1950s Franco used to spend the summer holidays with his brothers and sisters in a *casa cantoniera* set on a deserted stretch of road way up in the mountains some ten miles out of Castelbuono. *Case cantoniere* were houses built for maintenance road workers and their families – crimson painted two-storey, severely symmetrical stone buildings with a front door dead centre and plain square windows. You still see them all over Sicily in the most isolated and out-of-the-way places. With mechanised road maintenance the figure of the solitary worker with his pick and wheelbarrow gradually disappeared, and the houses fell into disuse; they're nearly all empty and abandoned now. I find them magical places, crumbling slowly away on their own in the silence of the Sicilian mountains.

For city children, being able to run wild, swim in the rivers and play with the children of the local peasants, made life in the *casa cantoniera* pure heaven. One day Franco and his brother discovered the white manna liquid oozing from the bark of a tree. They stuck their fingers in and licked them. They licked on and on and on. It gave them raging diarrhoea, and they never tried it again.

We went back to find the *casa cantoniera* one Autumn day. After you leave Castelbuono the road winds round and upwards into the quiet deserted mountains through woods of ash, olive and evergreen oak. The landscape is smoky grey-green, stretching up and away over peaks and valleys into the distance and appearing at a slightly different angle at each bend in the road. The air is clean and cool.

Franco catches a first glimpse of the house long before we get there; it appears for a split second amongst the trees and is gone again. It won't reappear until two or three more bends. The road runs downwards now and we bump over a stone bridge in a steep gulley; there's not much water in the river beneath, just a brown trickle running over a rock-strewn bed between banks which are thick and bulging with autumn vegetation.

Up steeply again and round, past two massive oaks and a solitary date palm. Far away on the top of one of the distant mountain peaks is a village looking like a dollop of chopped hazelnuts and cream. You can just make out a tower rising from the misty blur of ochre and white. A bell tower perhaps or part of the castle ramparts.

These hilltop towns and villages are still the only centres of habitation in the Madonie. Built as inaccessibly as possible in Medieval times to escape invaders, they are picturesque, scantily populated and freezingly cold in winter.

I was shocked when we stopped in front of the *casa cantoniera* to see what a state it was in: a pale ghostly red still covered the stone walls, but they were pitted and riddled with what looked liked bullet holes. There was still some glass in the upper windows but the eaves were hanging dangerously overhead and the roof was falling to bits,in fact the whole place looked decidedly unsafe. The heavy wooden front door was jammed,its hinges choked by grass and weeds, and a huge fig tree outside had its branches pressed hard against the downstairs windows so you couldn't get in that way either. We went round to the back, pushing through waist high undergrowth and raising a cloud of moths and craneflies.

A smooth stone platform overlooking the valley used to extend out from the back door where the grown-ups would sit out in the evenings and talk. There was no electricity then (and there still isn't) so a paraffin lamp would be placed on the long deal table, gently smoking in the night air. The platform had more or less subsided now beneath nettles but you could see what a magical place it must have been.

I wanted to see inside the house and find something from the family's past. The kitchen which I finally managed to get into by forcing back the splintered broken shutters and climbing over the window sill, was dank and gloomy. It had branches and leaves and sweet decaying figs littering the floor and a broken table with a scrap of blue and cream oilcloth still glued to it. When I stooped my head to go deeper into the house there was a flurrying of something living and winged. A bat flapped wildly up into my face.

You get a feeling in houses that have been taken over by nature that you're not wanted there any more. There was definitely something in the kitchen that day trying to push me away and quite clearly telling me not to go on into any of the other rooms. The sensation was so strong that I immediately turned round and climbed back through the kitchen window. What I might have found inside or upstairs on the first floor, I don't know.

Franco, who hadn't followed me into the house wanted to leave at once. On the way back to Palermo he told me that the landscape of the Madonie mountains hadn't changed at all since his childhood. It's heartbreakingly beautiful, smelling of flowers and wild grasses and there are no human beings anywhere.

12
Ms Rampling

I wonder whether the British actress Charlotte Rampling who is married to a Frenchman has similar problems to me. France after all is not all that different from Italy; they're both Latin countries notorious for their appalling bureaucratic machinery, and the French, just like the Italians, are obsessed with the workings of their bodies. Unlike them though, they're grumpy, and don't like the English all that much.

But Charlotte Rampling is slim and sophisticated and successful and she's married to a well-known man in films. She also lives in Paris, a city with a magic ring about it, which Palermo hasn't got. Does she have problems with her in-laws I wonder or with her husband's stomach complaints? You wouldn't think so looking at these photos of her. Charlotte Rampling is chic in a simple black designer dress and says she's taken up photography. I think she must be one of those women who turn back at the smart end of Via Ruggero Settimo – Rue di Faubourg St. Honoré in her case– to avoid the seedy, and who are never seen in state hospitals. I should love to get her on her own and ask her what she thinks about foreign men.

"What do you think about foreign men, Ms Rampling?"

"Do you ever get fed-up with living abroad?"

Even if she does, it's quick and easy to get from Paris to London, especially if you're monied and successful. It's longer and more expensive from here.

"What do you do when things break down or don't work or drive you mad Ms Rampling?"

"Do you ever wish you'd married an Englishman?"

"Do you consider the French to be a race of lunatics?"

I want to know what a sophisticated Englishwoman living abroad does when a drain overflows and nobody comes to mend it. I *must* know.

When I noticed filthy water cascading down past our front entrance for three successive days and nothing being done about it, I followed it to its source. Expatriation I keep telling myself as I trace the stinking stream, was surely never meant to be like this. The stinking stream led me to a blocked drain in one of the mean alleyways behind our building. I rang the municipal health offices. "There's a blocked drain in Via Tondino sending filthy water down our road. I'm seriously worried from a health point of view".

This was no good at all as any Sicilian (and probably Charlotte Rampling's husband) will tell you. You just don't call public departments on the phone for the very good reason that a disembodied voice being polite carries no weight whatsoever. On the contrary, it classifies you as a fool, good game for the bored clerk at the other end of the line. I was told I'd have to come into the office.

Knowing they'd insist on a written complaint, I had prepared one beforehand. It went like this:

> I, the undersigned.... born in..... on........,
> resident in........and domiciled at.....number...
> flat......staircase....fiscal number.... Hereby
> complain that:
>
> The drain situated in........ Street,
> two hundred metres from the building where
> I reside, flat.....number.....staircase......, has been
> overflowing for one week, i.e. from.......to...
> (day,month,year).
>
> I hearby demand that the competent
> authorities deal with the said drain immediately
> as the effluent presents a grave health risk to all
> those in the vicinity.
>
> Signed, dated and authenticated

Husbands regard their English wives witheringly when they go on crusades like this, but I had to prove to myself that things *could* get done through the legitimate channels if only you stick at it long enough. The drain was going to be unblocked. I was shunted around the corridors and rooms of the municipal offices, listened to in polite disbelief and finally relieved of my written complaint by a balding employee who smelt.

"This will be seen to as soon as possible" he assured me placing it in a desk drawer.

"The drain's unhealthy" I said again.

"Absolutely so."

"How long will it be before you can come and fix it?"

"Not long, not long. Within the week."

It was eventually fixed, but only because I cheated by telling a local councillor about it.

"They said a foreign woman had already been in" he told me a day or so later unable to keep the admiration from his voice. "They knew about it."

Then there were the broken railings. A car driven by a drunk driver had rammed them one night, waking me up with a tremendous crunching of masonry and splintering of glass. The iron railings which are nicely curlicued in places and probably quite valuable now, run along both sides of the artificially raised road outside our front entrance.

The road is really a stone viaduct which carries traffic up towards Monte Pellegrino and spans a narrow track below. Two of the curved arches down there have been illegally bricked-in and used as storerooms by people in nearby houses. Cars are parked under the others.

This extraordinary structure put up in the 1930s during Mussolini's government must be extremely resilient, although it vibrates alarmingly when a bus or loaded lorry drives over it. Whenever this happens pedestrians find themselves bouncing slowly up and down as though on a springboard. It's not a wholly unpleasant sensation – rather sensual in fact – yet I never feel *quite* safe there.

The damage done to the railings was dangerous as well as unsightly, with twisted and broken iron bars overhanging cars and people below. Great chunks of masonry had fallen off too. Although there is a nursery school down there nobody seemed in the least worried.

Someone must have done something though for one day when I got home, there were taut strips of red and white plastic fluttering over the missing bits of railing.

They are still there over a year later – as are the lumps of bridge poised ready to fall on our heads and kill us. I'm reminded when things like this happen of friends in Cumbria who complained about a dry stone wall outside their property where one stone had got dislodged. The wall was unsightly they said. The authorities came to replace it within the hour.

"And Ms Rampling......."

13
Let there be light

I knew about S.A.D. long ago before it became a recognised condition. S.A.D or Seasonal Affective Disorder is a profound state of lethargy and depression caused by lack of bright daylight which, doctors say, can be alleviated and even cured, by exposure to bright light. I would guess that 1950s London produced a glut of S.A.D. sufferers although I've no way of knowing. I look back for instance on an entirely black-and-white world – no colour at all. It's not an altogether unpleasant place to be, simply a drab one. There are lots of clouds and buildings and Victorian tiled roofs which either glisten gunmetal grey in the rain or sit silently under snow.

I was not a S.A.D. sufferer myself, being made melancholic rather than depressed by low cloud. But I did feel a physical need for bright hot sunshine and strong colours – Johnson's happier climates and fragrant gardens. I think it's a lovely twist that after I'd left London, it immediately became swinging and bursting with life and colour.

Once here of course, the impact was terrific; a sledgehammering glare of searing Mediterranean light. I wonder if Sicilians suffer from a reverse condition – D.A.S. maybe, or a surfeit of brightness. Perhaps they have to gaze into a crate of coal to feel better.

Everything dazzled the eye; there were brilliant yellow lemons everywhere, not the mean little specimens like dried-up testicles you get in

England, but luminous globes which covered the trees like children's drawings. Lemons are left to fall to the ground and rot in Sicily for there are too many of them. There are too many oranges as well. I remember discovering a dump one spring day in the middle of deserted countryside – tens of thousands of them which had obviously been tipped off a truck and left to slide and slither down the bare hillside. They lay there in a heap at the bottom like some beautiful but shameful secret.

As the light is so intense in Sicily, the nights seem very black indeed. There is no dusk to speak of and no long summer evenings. This is good for the open-air cinemas or *arene* which can open their doors in June and July from 8.30pm onwards. Lucky people whose blocks of flats back onto the cinemas can bring their supper out onto their balconies and watch the film for free, so a great deal of clattering of crockery and boisterous conversation goes on too. To add to the strangeness and charm of the *arene* there are the lizards who invariably scuttle across the screen or suddenly freeze mid-way on an actor's face like some evil boil.

It's very Sicilian to stand up and put your coats on the moment the film is over. In all the years I have been in Palermo I have never been able to read the cast list or credits.

"Will you please sit down!" hissed at the lady in front earns me an astonished stare. What *does* she want, The film's over, isn't it?

Another infuriating custom is not letting the cinema empty before the next lot come in. There are no regulations requiring you to wait in orderly silence in the foyer until the film is over and queueing is quite out of the question. So people congregate right outside the auditorium, talking very loudly so you miss the final crucial twist of the film. The moment they hear the closing music, in they surge like a heard of buffalo.

"Quick Beppe! Over here!" and a coat is flung over my seat before I have vacated it.

"Look, do you mind? I'm still here."

"Sorry Signora. Beppe, quick! They're two places here!"

By now the cinema is one heaving mass, one half of us trying to get out, the other trying to muscle its way in. Outside in the foyer, the man in the box office sits calm and aloof over his sheaf of tickets.

Let there be light.

* * *

And there was light. We shot out of the tunnel into bright sunshine, a shimmering white sea on our left, the mountainside sweeping down to within a few feet of the car on our right.

For a good deal of the way from Palermo to Messina the road runs parallel to the single-track railway. You can of course travel by train if you really want to, but the only route for lorries and coaches bound for the ferry and the Italian mainland is by this road. There are no problems on the stretches of existing motorway but the motorway is incomplete and there are still several kilometres of winding coastal road to manoeuvre. The lorries drive very fast round the hairpin bends here and sway horribly I never feel at ease travelling behind one.

I can see how foreigners find it quaint and charmingly Italian that Palermo (pop. 1 million the island's main city and seat of the Regional Government) is connected to Messina (city, port and gateway to the rest of Italy, sitting on the Straits) by such a tenuous thread. This is brought home more forcibly when you look at the map of Sicily and see that this west-east coastal route is the most direct. There can be landslides along the road in winter and the train is notoriously awful, but unless you want to do the journey through the middle of the island via Catania, this is your only choice.

I love it, and don't care how long it takes or what time of the year it is. From the tacky Palermo suburbs to the first view of the Straits of Messina it's always magical.

The tunnel we had just emerged from was one of many that cut through the mountains. There would be a lot more before we arrived – a whole series of black holes coming one after another, gulping us in in greedy mouthfuls. Winding their way beneath the tons of stone and each several kilometers long, they have circular slowly turning fans hanging from the roofs inside which are meant to prevent you dying of suffocation.

We stopped at a tiny level crossing a few miles out of Cefalù. The gatekeeper's house was built on the other side of the track on the edge of a narrow strip of land which fell steeply down to the sea. I could smell the geranium bushes in the hot, dry patch of front garden. There was dead silence and nothing happened for the next five minutes except the few cars coming to a halt behind us. Two pairs of jeans and a bathing costume hung motionless on a washing line.

I knew when the train was coming because the gatekeeper put on a scarlet peaked cap and began pulling levers. This was a ritual I'd seen before. In

the little village further along this coast where we used to rent a house, our next-door neighbour worked for the railways. I don't exactly know what her job was but every time the train was due into the tiny station there, she and her colleagues would don caps, and take them off again once the train had passed. The rules must have stipulated correct dress, though who was to notice I don't know.

And here was the train now. It cantered by over the rails: der-*dah*, der-*dah*, revealing four blank faces behind the windows. Then the keeper's wife raised the red and white barrier by laboriously turning a handle, and we crossed the tracks. The road ran so near the water's edge here that the shingle beach was only a couple of feet from my outstretched hand. A seagull sat preening its feathers on a huge rock. There is a seagull sitting on that same rock every time I pass.

We were nearly at the turning for Castelbuono where I had first seen the *casa cantoniera* and the manna trees. Away from us the road wound up and away into thickly wooded mountains. It looked mysterious and inviting. A few miles further along the main road we came to the village where we used to spend the summer months. I could see our house high up the spit of land running out to sea. The railway goes straight under this promontory, the train rushing into the tunnel with a roar right beneath the house, sending the furniture into a frenzy of shaking, and emerging again by now quite docile, in the village square.

Dark-light, dark-light.

It is an odd village – neither pretty nor ugly – inhabited by a cluster of slow-moving elderly people who sit outside their houses and watch the coming and going of August visitors in silent puzzlement. We rented a narrow two-storey village house wedged against others exactly like it on the promontory. One side overlooked the spectacularly beautiful sea and coastline as far as Cefalù while the back part gave onto a little square shut off at the end of the spit of land by an ancient castle. The pitted walls of the castle were full of housemartins' nests, and the birds would scream back and forth over our heads every evening at dusk.

Our landlady would have to be classified as mean – there wasn't even a doorknob on the front door – yet I couldn't help admiring her quite majestic parsimony. I think she was known for it throughout the village. When you pronounced her name, there was a short silence and then the subject would be changed. The fridge she provided was a rusty old horror which she refused to substitute.

"It works, doesn't it?"

"Well yes, but it's all rusty and cracked. Look."

"No, no," she'd shake her head, "nothing wrong with that at all."

And the dreadful bent knives and forks, the broken pane of glass in the downstairs bedroom window, the lumpy mattresses.

"I've cleaned the house for you" she would say when we arrived in July, "everything's in order."

I couldn't dislike her; she had terrible arthritis which I think may have been the cause of her grumpiness. She also owned the finest rooftop terrace in the whole village – higher up than anybody else's and with an uninterrupted view north, south, east and west over mountains, cliffs and sea.

Nothing had changed. I even saw the same bemused faces staring at us over their beers and card games at the roadside café.

By the time we got to Tindari, the tunnels were coming thick and fast. Tindari has a black Madonna sitting in a sanctuary at the top of a mountain (a "prodigious hillock" as my guidebook describes it) and strangely shaped sea lagoons below. The black-skinned statue is said to have arrived on a foreign boat which had sought shelter in the little bay during a storm. The only way the sailors could get the boat on its way again once the bad weather had passed, was by lightening its load and leaving the statue behind on the shore. This was was seen as a sign, and the Madonna has been venerated there ever since.

As for the lagoons, I have no idea how they were formed. They are extremely strange and beautiful – pools of deep blue pressed into kidney shapes or pulled out like chewing gum into long wobbly curves and crescents in the blindingly white sands. You can't gaze on them without longing to be down there in their silky waters. Actually they are as stagnant and still as moon pools and not really pleasant to swim in. Far better to go beyond them and slip into the open crystal sea.

By now we were on the last leg of the journey and climbing steadily. The final series of tunnels (roof fans functioning intermittently) opened suddenly out into the cool mountain air and we were rushing along the motorway on high stilts. Ahead and in the distance was the mainland with the ferries slowly criss-crossing the Straits of Messina.

14
Captain Bland from Yorkshire

Who was Henry Bland? His grave stands beautifully tended so somebody must care about him. But then, all the graves and paths here are kept neat and tidy with no weeds or dead flowers anywhere. All the merit of two dedicated employees of Palermo's Municipal Superintendence of Cemeteries who lovingly look after this foreigners' graveyard in the Vergine Maria area of Palermo. One of the men spent many years in America and enjoys speaking English, the other is quiet and wears a woolly cardigan. They're both saddened by the fact that so few people visit the graves.

"We often say prayers for the people here" they told me, "so their souls don't feel lonely."

The bodies here are the non-Catholics or non-Sicilians who for one reason or another ended their days on the island – Germans, Frenchman, Jews and Britons.

> In affectionate remembrance of Captain Henry Bland
> of Scarborough, Captain of S.S. Harelda who died at sea
> December 19th 1879 aged 44 years.

A simple vertical slab and a Celtic cross. What did he die of? Scurvy perhaps, or did the *Harelda* go down in dangerous currents off the coast; where was she bound for and what was she carrying? Did any other members of the crew die and who took over from Captain Bland? Further back lies another British seaman:

> He died in HMS Resistance through
> falling from aloft. 13 October 1865.

What a death.

There must have been other disasters round the Sicilian coasts during the eighteenth and nineteenth centuries although there's not much evidence of them here. The ratings, able seamen and cabin boys who lost their lives either in wrecks or accidents on board may well lie in another neglected and inaccessible graveyard further down the road near the sea shore. An isolation hospital used to here in the sixteen-hundreds so it's reasonable to suppose the adjacent cemetery was built for victims of contagious diseases. Any seamen, passengers (and probably goods as well) who arrived in the port of Palermo from infected areas in the world could be immediately quarantined in the hospital. Those who succumbed could then be buried quickly and unceremoniously next door. The sooner the better.

The Inghams would have been here in Sicily at the time Henry Bland died. Like the unfortunate captain, the Inghams were Yorkshiremen; unlike him they lived and prospered. It was Benjamin Ingham, originally from Ossett, who arrived in Sicily in 1806 hoping to boost sales of the family business of cotton and woollen textiles. And with a staggering 17,000 British troops stationed on the island at the time, he stood a fair chance of succeeding. From 1806 in fact, until 1815, Sicily was under British rule; not a long period maybe, but one of the island's richest. Benjamin, who had been thrown over by a girlfriend in Huddersfield and got involved in an unsuccessful business venture, swore he wouldn't return to England until he had made enough money to buy up the whole of Ossett.

Once over here, he discovered the commercial value of practically every Sicilian product from sulphur, liquorice and citrus fruit to pumice and manna. But it was marsala which made his fortune. The potential of this delicious dessert wine – not unlike madeira in appearance and taste – had already begun to be exploited by another expatriate Englishman, John Woodhouse. Having made the most of his friendship with Admiral Nelson, Woodhouse was now happily supplying the British fleet with barrels of the stuff.

After he had been on the island some fourteen years, Ben Ingham joined forces with another Yorkshire family, the Whitakers, whom he was related to by marriage. Excited by tales of the fabulous opportunities awaiting him in Sicily, Ben's nephew Joseph Whitaker sailed from England in 1820 and joined his uncle. Soon they were exporting the dark rich marsala to Britain and the United States.

Over the years these Yorkshire families intermarried with the Sicilians to produce a succession of Giuseppes, Tinas and Euphrosynes. They built sumptuous houses and gardens for themselves, becoming increasingly richer and more influential, travelling, holding salons and offering hospitality to visiting English and European royals. Villa Malfitano – a huge neo-Renaissance-style mansion filled with art treasures and surrounded by magnificent subtropical gardens was just one of their homes. An almost obscenely prolific wisteria spills down over the front wall, and inside, in the drawing room, a portrait of the old Queen Mary is perched regally on top of the grand piano.

It was in Villa Malfitano that the Queen's Birthday Party was celebrated one July by the British community. I wore a gorgeous emerald-green silk dress I remember, and only wished Harold could have seen me as I flitted royally through the dwarf palms and vermilion hibiscus.

These occasions are so quintessentially British that young Sicilian husbands must feel decidedly ill-at-ease among the HM consuls and dry sherries. Yet for others, like the English-Speaking Ladies' Coffee Morning group, the QBP represented the highlight of the whole year.

Long tables had been laid out in the gardens under the balustraded terrace and drinks were being dispensed by white-jacketed waiters. Guests drove up the sweeping driveway in the gathering dusk, leaving their cars under the enormous *ficus magnolioides* tree at the side of the house. Here they would be greeted by the consul and his wife before making their way towards the drinks.

There was always the same batch of Sicilian authorities present: the chief of police, the incumbent army general, the head of the fire brigade and so on, as well as representatives from the other foreign consulates in Palermo. The Prefect was also invited but didn't always show up. The Italian bigwigs who did attend, did so naturally enough with their wives. Formal party-going of this kind is a funny business and I always got the impression that the British effort was considered the most splendid and the most prestigious among Palermo ladies. Certainly they were always immaculately attired. But then so were we.

The food was very good that year I remember so the consular coffers must have been full (in the leaner years we just got mass-produced cocktail snacks). A rich buffet soon appeared, and sufficiently oiled with alcohol by then to dispense altogether with good manners, we surged towards the tables.

An Englishman I dislike began talking in a very loud voice as he reached across me for a pile of the fish risotto:

"How're things, eh? All right, eh? Good do, eh?"

He gave the most dreadful laugh and started elbowing his way in. There was a massive crush round the tables now, so that our silks, chiffons and gold-chained handbags got all caught up in an inelegant twist. Sweat ran off shiny faces, make-up ran in the humid summer evening.

"*Prego signora, un po' di focaccia agli spinaci?*"

Spinach flan..Why not?

"*Insalata di funghi? Pollo alla maionese? Salmone..bresaola?*"

Yes, pile it on. In for a penny....

Near the fountain at the foot of the sweeping flight of stone steps stood a portly Italian naval officer in white and gold, hands behind his back, eyeing me. The Sicilians don't really enjoy social drinking and invariably leave these parties sober and, I would think, pretty bored. His expression reminded me of the dreaded Alfredo of the old Berlitz days.

A clap of hands, or was it a pastry fork tapping on a glass?

"Ladies and Gentlemen; *Signore e Signori*, raise your glasses please to Her Majesty Queen Elizabeth the Second!"

"THE QUEEN!"

Unhappily, when the Consulate closed down – taking my job with it – the supply of caviare and champers abruptly dried up and these delightful parties were no more.

Two of the people always present at British cocktail parties were Terry and Rex. Both had been stationed in Sicily during the war and both stayed on. I don't think they had much to do with each other apart from meeting on these social occasions. But then they were very different.

Rex had married a Sicilian baroness. He had been part of the Palermo-based Allied government under General Patton and after the war had served as Vice-consul. A large, cultured and rather clumsy man, he spoke an atrociously accented Italian. Terry was from the industrial north of England. I worked with him at the Consulate when he was vice-consul. He had had very little formal education and I imagine had been quite poor, but had managed to work his way up through the notoriously snobby consular environment to become liked and respected by everyone. He also become an expert on shipping affairs which formed quite an important part of consular work then.I was very fond of him; he was entirely without malice or guile. He too married a Sicilian.

Rex lent me a book written by a fellow officer of his. It was a diary written during the Allied government period in Palermo. The officer had been an anthropologist and was fascinated by the unusual physical characteristics of Sicilians; blue eyes with black hair – that sort of thing.

"He used to stop in the middle of the street" Rex told me, "and point to somebody in front: "just look at the shape of that head", he'd say, "isn't that *amazing*?"

Although I never came across her at the Villa Whitaker consular parties, I do remember catching sight of the tiny bent figure of the elderly and frail Delia Whitaker – the last surviving Sicilian-based member of the dynasty – in church. Someone who knew her was my own Harold Acton. Writing about a tea party he attended in 1944 (in Rome I think it was) he remarks how although Delia looked extremely old – as old in fact as her mother – she continued to be treated by her as a child. The "child" was 59 at the time which seems rather unkind a fate.

Delia died in 1971, but not before creating the Whitaker Foundation to preserve Villa Malfitano and the tiny island of Motya. This mysterious and silent patch of land lying in a lagoon off the Trapani coast was bought by their family and especially loved by one of the Giuseppes who enjoyed excavating a Phoenician port and a burial ground there.

The presence of the Whitakers is still felt in Palermo. The Anglican church of the Holy Cross for instance where a British chaplain still officiates, was built by Joseph Whitaker in 1872. Too late to receive the soul of the nameless seaman who fell to his death aboard *HMS Resistance*, but in time perhaps to hold a service in memory of Captain Henry Bland.

* * *

Both Franco and I only just made it to the end of the war. I almost bowed out in London when a V-2, one of the German rocket-powered missiles fell just up the road from us in West Hampstead. People always knew when these were about to come down because the engine would suddenly cut out.

"This is it, darling" my father said to my mother as the approaching roar of the rocket went abruptly and terrifyingly silent right overhead. A second or two later there was a tremendous explosion which blew in all the windows of the flat and showered my cot pillow with glass. My distraught mother found me still asleep and quite unharmed.

Here in Palermo, Franco's family were living temporarily in a top-storey flat just off the central Via Amari. They were continually on the move to be near my father-in-law, a colonel who taught in a military academy in the north of Italy. In 1939 his wife brought her four children down to Palermo where her fifth, Franco, was soon to be born, then, three years later my father-in-law was sent to Russia at the head of the 278th Infantry Regiment. Tragically, he was never to return from the disastrous campaign there. There is now a street in Palermo named after him.

Via Amari sweeps straight down to the port and I don't suppose the family had any idea how severely the area was to be targetted by the enemy. One day, there was a particularly thunderous explosion which shook the entire building. Anna, my mother-in-law, snatched up the new baby in panic and wrenched open the front door of their top-floor flat. She already had one foot outside before realising that the whole house had been sliced cleanly in half by a bomb and there was nothing underneath her. Ignazia the maid, grabbed hold of her clothes just in time.

The Americans landed in Sicily three months later in July 1943; Patton had a tablet put up in the English church:

> To the glory of God. In memory of the heroic
> Americans of the Seventh Army and the supporting
> units of the Navy and Air Force who gave their
> lives for victory in the Sicilian campaign. July
> 10 – August 17 1943. From their General.

War damage is still visible around the port and unexploded bombs are very occasionally found there. One was uncovered earlier this year during road works.

15
The strain of being chic

My appointment was at nine-thirty; Mario's daughter opened the door and took my jacket.

"Just take a seat for a few moments, will you?"

Mario's is particularly palatial; he had the whole place done out with fake pink and beige marble wallpaper some years back which sounds awful but in fact is so well-done it looks real. His own corner has a pseudo-antique oak console resting on oriental pug-dog legs and a framed mirror standing on the top. There is a scalloped onyx ashtray there too where he puts the lighted cigarettes he never manages to finish. The row of armchairs under the windows are pearl grey and the three-piece suite where you wait is upholstered in striped scarlet and cream satin. When you perch on its unyielding surface and glance sideways, you can see yourself reflected in the floor-to-ceiling mirrors at each end.

There's a bar in the corner with a curved maroon counter top where they'll make you a cup of coffee, and nearby a rack of glossy magazines; the local paper, the *Giornale di Sicilia* is always on the heavy glass coffee table too if you prefer that. I like the windows running down one side; they have thick-stemmed succulents and geraniums planted in the long plant troughs outside their sliding panes. Beyond, you can look down over the moving stream of traffic to the park on the other side of the road.

I was called. I got up and walked past the ebony and gold blackamoor poised on his plinth to the three steps at the other end.

"Good morning Signora, would you like to sit here?"

Now I can lie back and admire the way the concealed lighting bathes the smooth cream ceiling in a gentle glow and glistens on the shelves of bottles and jars.

"That all right for you?"

"Fine, thank you."

It is pleasant and relaxing; I close my eyes for five minutes.

"Right, there we are, now if you'd just like to come with me.."

Mario is waiting. We've known each other for years and years but still use the polite form of address when we speak. In Italian this means using the pronoun *lei* instead of *tu* when you say "you" (*and* making all the wretched verbs in the sentence agree). I'd like to use the familiar form with him but somehow know I couldn't. Saying *ciao* to Mario just wouldn't do.

Mario worries about his thinning hair; he once asked me to investigate a doctor in London who had discovered a cure for making it grow back again. I spent quite a lot in postage getting all the details for him, but he got cold feet at the last moment.

He called over one of the girls to empty his ashtray. He keeps a large staff – about seven girls and a couple of boys – all dressed in monogrammed white tops. The boys are different every time I come, but always languid-looking and always spending their free moments twisting locks of hair around their fingers in front of the mirrors.

"Right Signora, what shall we do today?"

Mario knows everything about my hair; it's thick and heavy and he loves taking his scissors to it. It presents a challenge to his sculpturing technique. Hair in Italian is plural so I now have to say:

"My hairs have got so long, Mario, you know how fast they grow. Can't you do something really new with them today?"

This always sounds terribly obscene to me when I think about it, especially now, when he answers:

"Yes they certainly do. We could cut them and then brush them forwards over your...."

Oh God.

My visits to Mario are only one part of the strain of keeping chic in Palermo. I've already mentioned my expensive dentist, and this hairdresser's is not cheap. Then there is the beautician, the cosmetics and the clothes. All this goes against the grain of the home-grown Englishwoman who likes to be casual and comfortable.

"Why on earth do you bother so much?" I am asked when I go over to England, "you can wear anything here; nobody cares what you look like."

I know this, yet somehow feel I have to make the effort. Italian women are so very formal and some of this has rubbed off on me. My next-door neighbour for instance, wouldn't dream of taking the rubbish downstairs without her shoulder pads in. When I'm working I'm properly turned-out, (it's the only time I can afford to be); when I'm not, or when I'm at home writing, I don't bother.

Palermo used to be considered the chic-est and most elegant of the Italian cities. Franco always had his shirts and suits made-to-measure because the tailors here were so brilliant and not over-expensive, and the results beautiful. I had my clothes tailor-made too in the early days. My Irish flatmates and I would troop off to the Rizzo brothers near Via Ruggero Settimo and have costumes, dresses and trousers made for ourselves. It was an entirely new experience.

The Rizzos' clothes were superbly cut and sewn and looked gorgeous on. We all tried to be very Continental by choosing quiet pearl greys and burnished browns for our clothes. Nothing over the top. No frills.

One of the brothers – the butchier, round-headed one – was for the men, the other, thinner and aesthetic-looking, did the women's clothes. I had a lovely pair of trousers made by the ladies' tailor – a slim-fitting pair in soft chocolate-brown wool. I'll never forget standing in his fitting rooms in front of the mirror while he knelt on the the floor and gently inserted pins into my crotch with his long white fingers. I felt everything and he knew it.

My clothes now are off the peg – when I can afford it from my favourite Italian label. There are places here of course where a T-shirt will cost two hundred thousand lire (£80 odd). Is it any better than a M&S one? Yes, it's in a different class. Can spending like that be justified? No.

The shinier the window, the more expensive the stuff inside. To protect themselves and their wares, most shops in this class have locked doors and you have to press a bell to get in. Sometimes it's enough just to peer through the glass for the door to be opened by the smart and eagerly smiling assistant. Thank God, a customer.

It would be wrong to say all Palermo women are chic; the ones in my *borgata* for instance, come to their front doors to buy a cauliflower from the

travelling greengocer in their dressing gown and slippers. I don't think they bother to get dressed at all sometimes. But the majority of women want to be immaculate at all times of the day.

My smart friend Titti – the one I had seen that evening at the Gibellina theatre – told me about her beautician.

"She's not cheap mind you, but she'll tell you exactly what you need. Go and see her."

I was put in a sort of chair when I got there, and tipped right back until I was staring at the ceiling. Then a large circular magnifying glass was pulled forward over my face and the Signora peered through it. I had blackheads between my eyebrows she said, and ageing skin, and was I ready was the full facial cleansing?

I said I hadn't really thought of having that done and perhaps I could just have some products this time.

I paid an inordinate amount for a cream wash, a day moisturiser and a revitalising tonic.

"Are you sure this will help?" I asked the Signora.

"Look at me." She got hold of my wrist, pulled up her cotton top and ran my hand over the skin on her chest.

"There, feel how smooth that is" she said "Eh? What d'you think?"

"Yes..."

"You keep on using my products, Signora," she said "and then we'll see."

I did keep it up for a good six months and tried to persuade myself I could see an improvement. I *think* I look better but I'm not really sure.

Women here tend to be fanatical about keeping their bodies trim and firm too; there are gyms all over the city. There's one near me in a basement garage opposite the photographer's. The enthusiastic owner (who is also the photographer) got an artist to do a mural on the white wall running down one side of the sloping drive to the entrance. It was extremely good: three or four life-size figures in various stages of physical exertion. There was a Japanese karate exponent leaping into the air, a fencer, and a beautiful girl in low-cut leotard and tights kicking one leg very high into the air. It was obvious as soon as the brightly-coloured paintings appeared that there was going to be trouble with the high-kicking girl. Sure enough, after a few days an arrow and a rude little sign appeared between her legs. This was painted out but has reappeared so many times in differing versions since, that now there is a just a blur beneath her waist.

One would have to spend so much time inside a gym to work off the fat accumulated by Sicilian snacks and pizzas. At Marziano's bakery for instance, they do the most wonderful takeaway pizza portions which I just can't resist.

Marziano's has got so popular over the years that they have had to introduce a system of numbered tickets for their pizzas. This replaced the previous state of anarchy in which you had to fight your way through the crowds and bellow your order to the girl behind the counter. It's only marginally better now, as the crowds are the same and you have to strain your ear above the din to hear your number called. The delightful couple who run the bakery keep absolutely calm throughout this mayhem – the husband hurrying up the orders, the wife going flat-out at the till. Neither of them ever lose their temper or get flustered. I am always given a big smile by the husband, being recognised as the customer who once called another woman a bulldozer. It happened when an enormous signora was pushing me from behind as I waited at the till, almost squashing the breath out of me. I turned round and let her have it. The word "bulldozer" which is the same in Italian (pronounced *booll-dotser*) had an immediate impact. The woman was so taken aback at being compared to an earthmover that she collapsed in on herself and fell back silently into the crowd like a spent balloon.

Marziano's bakery is in a narrow one-way street in which parking is forbidden. This doesn't stop customers (ourselves included) from leaving their cars triple-parked while they nip in for bread and pizzas. And what pizzas! Look at them inside their rectangular metal trays, steaming and bubbling straight from the ovens, carried head-high by bakers clad in white singlet and shorts, faces streaming with sweat. The trays are plonked down on trestle tables, emptied, taken away and replaced almost immediately.

"Fifty-four!"

That's me. "Here!"

"What d'you want, Signora?"

Quick, quick I must decide! The furious pace at Marziano's gives you no time for hesitation or muzzy thinking.

"Well, Signora?"

"Yes, well... I'll have three portions of the *rustico* and two of the....*margherita*. Oh, and two of the *sfincione*."

Celestial *sfincione* with its soft, spongey bread base and topping of oil-soaked breadcrumbs, onion and tomato.

The girl seizes the pizza scissors and attacks one of the brimming trays. Lifting a fat strip onto a sheet of greaseproof paper on the scales, she yells out "Half a kilo!" before setting to on the *rustico*. This has thin slices of raw tomato and salami on top and is gooey with mozzarella.

Once outside on the milling pavement with our steaming packet we find somebody has parked behind our car so we can't get out. We hoot continuously, outraged at such effrontery until the owner arrives with an apologetic smile, a Latin spread of the hands and his bunch of keys.

* * *

The first heat of the showjumping competition the other afternoon was won by Andrea Fucks of Switzerland. Her name appeared in huge red letters on the electronic scoreboard,

ANDREA FUCKS

I couldn't believe this and had to check in my programme. In fact her real name was Andrea Fuchs – they had just slipped up on the H.

The showjumping circuit is in the Favorita Park, not far from the municipal tennis courts where I used to play. It's very attractive with its semicircle of pine trees and the backdrop of Monte Pellegrino. They put banks of flowers all round the course for the October season.

I always think I should find it an interesting sport but get bored very quickly; nothing much ever seems to happen and even the riders look glum when they collect their cups at the end. I always hope there'll be some spectacular accident to liven things up. Apart from Miss Fucks, there were competitors from Spain, Austria, Germany and of course Italy, but none at all from Britain. That made it even more monotonous.

Palermo-based students try and get taken on for the few days of the showjumping championships as hostesses, interpreters or drivers to make a bit of extra cash. There's not an awful lot for them to do once they do get in; it's not a popular spectator sport here and the stands were almost empty when I went. Still, half a million lire pocket money is better than nothing. On the way home I was stopped by the *carabinieri*. They flagged me down just past the football stadium. In theory, these spot checks are no more than a nuisance as long as you're a law-abiding, tax-paying citizen and have an honest face. At least I always hope this is the case.

As usual they asked to see my driving license and registration papers. A young floury face peered in at me.

"You know Signora, you're the first person we've stopped today who's been wearing a seat belt."

Seat belts are compulsory in Italy.

"Well," I said trying to be funny, "you'll have handed out a lot of fines, then."

The young *carabiniere* smiled: "Eh no, we'd never get through the day's work if we did that." He frowned at my driving license," Where were you born?"

"It says there" I told him, "in London."

"Oh, so you're English" he said as if that explained everything – seat belts and all. You hardly expect Sicilians to respect every little rule and regulation, do you? It wouldn't be reasonable. But foreigners – well, they're disciplined – a different kettle of fish altogether. I felt he would have given me a ticket had I *not* been wearing a belt, just because I was English and should have known better.

Just past the football stadium where I had been stopped, there's a gypsy encampment: a piece of wasteland the town council has put at the disposal of the hundreds of nomadic peoples who flood into southern Italy. Although it is behind a high stone wall, you can still get a glimpse of their caravans, tents and washing lines as you join the main road from the Favorita park.

To the casual visitor, the gypsy women look very picturesque; they wear flowered skirts down to their ankles which swish as they stride along, and have coloured scarves on their head. Their skin is dark and they have gold teeth and hanks of bleached hair. Either you never see their menfolk or these look no different from the Sicilians.

The women nearly always have sleeping babies cradled in their right arm, so they can use the left one for begging. They come up to you at the traffic lights with a piteous expression and outstretched hand, and if the car window is wound up they will tap on the glass until you look at them. Their babies tend to be tightly swaddled and you never hear a peep out of them. My theory is that they're kept up all night so that they're exhausted for the morning's begging stint and sleep right through it. They also almost certainly don't belong to the women who hold them. A friend of mine has noticed the same mother for a couple of years, yet the baby in her arms never gets any bigger.

It is common knowledge – the gypsies themselves have admitted as much – that begging is just part of a way of life – a game almost – played between themselves and the dumb public. If we are stupid enough to pay up, so much the worse for us. That's our problem. Gypsies do not really need alms; I've watched them get out of paying on the buses and seen them in the shops exchanging their coins for cakes and fags. I'm not sure where the gypsies in Palermo come from; they speak a vaguely slav-sounding language so I imagine from central or Eastern Europe. I never used to bother much about them until two things made me change my mind.

The first was a story told me by someone who had been accosted by two gypsy women while she was shopping. They immediately began to talk to her very rapidly.

"As they spoke, I found a great wave of pity sweeping over me," she said, "they were telling me how poor they were and how they suffered. I opened my purse and gave them everything I had, feeling I wanted to be as generous as I possibly could. I wanted them to have everything."

It was only when they'd gone that she realised what had happened – that she had been nothing less than hypnotised. I heard of a similar case very soon afterwards, only this time a man had actually taken the gypsies back to his flat and given them everything – money, jewellery and even (I think) his pension book.

The other incident concerned me and happened to me a few years ago. I had just got back from America and was feeling very odd with jet lag. One morning there was a ring at the door; outside were two gypsies. I don't remember now whether they had a baby with them, but I think they probably did. Instead of holding out her hand for money, one of the women asked whether she could have a glass of water. I immediately felt that of course she should have a glass of water – that that was the least I could give her.

I got it and watched her while she drank. Then she said she'd read my hand. I said no, I didn't want her to do that, there was no need – I didn't want any payment as it were for the water, and I made a gesture as if to close the door. But she insisted. Again, I can't remember whether she actually took my palm or whether she delivered what she had to say simply by looking at me. Her Italian was very strange and I couldn't understand everything, but the gist of what she told me was this:

Somebody was envious of me, of what I had achieved and wanted to harm me. But this person wouldn't succeed because I was in the grace of God. (Or somebody, somewhere was protecting me.)

I didn't know what to make of all this, but it upset me in an indefinable way. The result was that following the gypsies' visit, I spent the oddest and perhaps one of the most disturbing periods of my life. I stayed awake for one entire night, unable even to keep lying down, and I became worried sick about something I'd just had published. Then, after a week or so it was all over and things returned to normal. You could say it was all due to a particularly bad case of jet-lag, and it might well have been. On the other hand I did have inklings from a very unexpected quarter that someone had resented some modest achievement of mine.

Besides gypsies, there is a whole band out there waiting to pounce. The other day I was cleaning the bathroom when the downstairs buzzer went. I picked up the entry phone:

"Yes?"

"Signora, the Bible is all-truthful."

I was still holding the lavatory brush.

"Thank you, but I'm a bit busy at the moment. I'm sorry..."

"Signora, the Holy Word can change our lives. Have you ever thought how it can help you.....?"

Then there are the Jehovah's Witnesses and the Mormons. I must admit to being intrigued by these last ones. You always see them in pairs in their white shirts striding purposefully along the streets. I almost followed a couple of them once, so curious was I to see where they were going. What do they do in Catholic Sicily? Whither are they bound? Who do they manage to convert?

I once made the mistake of telling some Evangelists that "I was of a different faith", so it was useless their wasting time trying to convert me. It was the worst thing I could have said. "I am not a Catholic" acted like a carrot to them – a challenge.

"That is completely irrelevant Signora. What we should all do – all and every one of us, is open our ears and our eyes to the love of ....."

Non-religious but particularly annoying are the people who ring up trying to sell you revolutionary new methods for learning English. At the same time I'm terribly sorry for them – so young and desperately trying to make a bit of money.

"I'm afraid you've picked the wrong person here" I told one the other day, "I'm from London and we all speak perfect English in my family."

A perplexed silence: "yes, but it can always be useful. You see, this is a unique series of cassettes and books devised by a team of experts.." (I know what that means) "... with a special booklet giving you the chance to test yourself on..."

"I'm sorry, I'm really not interested."

Exit the team of experts. If they're anything like the inventors of some of the teaching material I've seen, it's better if they never see the light of day.

16
Obbs and obligations

Last night at a concert I saw the electrician. He lives in the tiny ground-floor flat in our block, a morose, half-crazed man with a black beard and staring eyes who ignores all the other people in the building. If he sees you coming home laden with shopping, he will bang the back entrance door in your face or mutter something under his breath. One of his pastimes is to take the plastic bin liner out of its container in our parking area and scatter its contents over the front hallway. Another is to smear residents' cars with mud. Passing his back window you occasionally hear him screaming at his wife, a little mouse of a woman who scurries everywhere with downcast eyes.

This is the man I saw last night at the concert. I was waiting in the foyer for a friend, and there a few feet in front of me, standing next to a potted palm, was the electrician. Not only was he dressed in an immaculate dark suit and tie with highly polished black shoes, he was also smiling and talking animatedly to another man. Strangest of all, he carried a violin case in his hand.

Now, this was one of the weekly concerts given by the Teatro Massimo Orchestra as part of their Autumn/Winter season. These events have a long and hallowed tradition and have always been attended by the same dedicated group of Palermo music lovers – for the most part, middle-aged, knowledgeable and rather snobby. That night the programme was Listz's first piano concerto in E flat major and Mozart's *Jupiter* Symphony, plus an unknown

Italian contemporary piece.

I felt I ought to go up to the electrician's companion, chatting so blithely away to him and say:

"I'm sorry to butt in like this, but do you realise the man you're talking to empties rubbish all over the place? I mean, do you realise he's round the bend? You can't possibly be having a proper conversation with a person like that."

I did nothing of the kind of course, just looked round the milling foyer. I recognised several faces – one of them belonging to a man I see sunbathing every year near our beach hut. It was the first time I had seen him with his trousers on.

This second sighting disconcerted me even further, but it was time to go to our seats. As I followed the other people into the auditorium I began vaguely wondering whether Harold Acton had ever come across a mad electrician at a symphony concert in Florence, and if he had, what his reaction would have been.

The soloist in the Liszt piece had recently won a prestigious award and gave a very accomplished performance. At the end, the woman in front of me jumped to her feet applauding hysterically and shouting for an encore. Actually they don't shout "encore!" in Italy, but "*bis!*" (pronounced bees). When the whole place gets going, it sounds most peculiar, as though the audience is hissing and booing instead of applauding.

Twice the soloist left the stage and twice he returned; the second time round he graciously acknowledged the bees, flung up his coat tails and sat down again at the piano.

The Chopin nocturne was beautifully played and sounded quite different to the way I do it. But then I'm not a professional musician. Piano playing for me is only one of my "obbs" as a neighbour of ours puts it. This neighbour once wanted to know what obbs Franco had. Fishing? Playing cards maybe?

Quite a bit of card-playing goes on down in our neighbourhood, usually on weekends, with two men playing and the rest crowding round to watch. It's an exclusively male obb, with the cards being furiously flung on to an upturned crate placed under the cherry laurel trees in the square.

I always think it looks so uncomfortable for them especially as the dry, beaten earth under the trees is dotted with sun-dried dog excrement. Still, nobody seems to pay much attention to comfort or to nice veiws in this part of Palermo. The benches for instance, which the local council have placed at intervals along the pavements are all positioned so that you sit facing a row of dustbins or parked cars.

The men play a game called *scopa* using the Italian pack of cards which is smaller and has different suits and figures from the English ones. I was always left out of family games of *scopa* because I could never remember the value of each card. You look down at your hand expecting to see a familiar jack of spades and instead there's this absurd man in doublet and hose holding a large gold coin.

The knot of old men playing cards in the square was one of the first things I noticed when I got back from England last summer; there they were, sitting in exactly the same place as when I left.

I had flown in from London on the usual charter flight, the one we've been using for years now. These companies which charter British aircraft were originally set up for Sicilian immigrants in Britain and their relatives. As the ticket costs half the price of the scheduled flight, this meant they could go backwards and forwards very cheaply at Christmas and during the summer holidays. Tickets were later made available to anybody else travelling between Britain and Sicily, and are now used by holiday operators as well.

There are disadvantages as well as advantages in using the charter. On the plus side, you have a good price and a direct London to Palermo flight instead of having to stop over in Rome or Milan; against, you don't have an exactly restful journey.

The Sicilians who first emigrated to Britain came from the poorest and most isolated villages on the island. Not only did they not speak English, they could hardly manage Italian either. I remember travelling next to tiny silent women and their bewildered husbands who had no idea what a seat belt was. They couldn't understand any of the announcements either. Once, on our way back, we were told (in English) that the plane couldn't land in Palermo because of high winds, and that it was going on to Malta. When we came down in Valetta, all the Sicilians thought they'd arrived in Palermo.

Things have moved on since then; the children and grandchildren of these first-generation immigrants have grown up in Britain and now travel regularly over to Sicily. Then there are the parties of schoolchildren and university students visiting London; there are holiday-makers, and there are the expatriates.

It is a notoriously rowdy flight, starting off with the joyful scrum round the check-in at Luton airport – it must be a real trial to air crews.

"Oh God Sue, they've put me on the Sicilian run this Saturday, I can't bear it."

"Oh poor you – I wish I could help, but I'm on Tenerife this weekend and then it's Monastir on Monday."

"I don't think I can get through another one of them, I really don't."

The real trouble is the Sicilians' nervous energy; they just cannot sit still on planes and have to walk up and down the whole time. They can't bear to wait for the duty free trolley to come to them but have to rush up to it as soon as it appears through the fore curtain. You can always tell you're on the Palermo-bound plane by the crowds milling in the aisle.

"Will you please sit down, sir" the hostess says with a tight smile, "we're bringing the drinks along now."

"Would you please sit down!" (slightly louder).

An announcement over the intercom in ghastly Italian:

"Would all passengers please remain IN THEIR SEATS while the crew are bringing the drinks round. Thank you."

"Please Miss, I would like two bottle of whisky and I want cigarettes Benson Edges"

"One minute, Madam..if you sit down, I'll see to you in a mom...."

"Benson Edges."

It's the same when we come into land. No matter how many times we are told to keep our seat belts fastened until the plane had come to a complete standstill, there is always a furious clicking accompanied by thunderous applause as soon as the wheels touch the tarmac. Students who have spent a fortnight in London are weeping with joy as Sicily hoves into view beneath them.

"No no Madam! Keep your belts fastened! No, we haven't come to a halt yet! For heavens sake Tracy, get them to sit down."

No good; before the incredulous stares of obedient British travellers on their *Discovery of Sicily Tour (Hidden Byzantine Treasures June/July; Magna Graecia Sept/Oct.)* the overhead compartments are snapped open. Bags and M&S carrier bags begin to rain down.

"I say Mildred, this is all rather extraordinary, isn't it? What do you think's happening?"

"No idea, sweetie. Perhaps it's always like this."

It is.

I come back from England laden with books which I never manage to read. I've counted thirty-four this time which I have to get through before my next trip over and the arrival of a fresh supply. I'm particularly worried about the three huge biographies waiting on the shelf: all "definite" and of all of "great scholarship".

And this is only the English reading. Italian novels and social criticisms also have to be tackled as well as a quick flick-through of the newspapers and weekend supplements. You have to keep up with things here too – it's part of being a Successful Expatriate.

Access to lending libraries in Palermo tends to be fraught with endless waiting and form-filling, so most of my research is done from a twenty-volume set of *New Age* Encyclopedia which I was sold many years ago by a brilliantly convincing door-to-door salesman. He had obviously got information from somewhere that I was English, for I don't see how he could possibly have flogged it to an Italian. *New Age* is very American with pages and pages on Wisconsin and Nebraska and – not surprisingly since it was printed in 1963 – delightful out-of-date illustrations. Still, it's got a lot of basic information which I can use.

When I pulled out volume 16 (Royal Ballet – Sofia) a small cockroach scuttled out of the pages dedicated to Sicily. It sat motionless for a moment on a black and white photograph of a *contadino* astride a mule in the village of Caccamo, and looked at me. A terrible glossy, crunchy brown, it waved its long feelers alternately up and down, trying to decide which way to escape. A piece of the *New Age* text caught my eye:

In addition to its exposure to volcanic eruption, Sicily suffers from earthquakes. Summers are almost rainless, since the sirocco, a dry, dusty wind, blows from North Africa across the island.

True, but how awful it sounded. Nobody would ever choose to come here after a description like that. The article, which went on to describe Sicily's history, was signed Norman J. G. Pounds, Indiana University. I wondered if Norman J. G. Pounds had been here himself, and if so, whether he had enjoyed it. Was he a fun-loving extrovert? It helps in Sicily if you are. Not being a naturally gregarious person myself, I sometimes think I should have chosen somewhere better suited to my temperament like Norway. One can't imagine the Norwegians rushing up and down the aisle on the London to

Oslo flight. They probably don't have cockroaches there either; it'd be too cold.

But then I don't like cold climates; I don't like large, shiny beetles either. That's why the island in the Indian Ocean where I went some years ago should have been the ideal place. I was staying on one of the Maldive islands, a beautiful tropical dot in a coral atoll some four hours by sea from the tip of Sri Lanka. There, all the unpleasant insects had been eliminated so that they wouldn't bother the tourists, in fact, every ten days or so, a trip would be organised to another island in the atoll leaving our own place empty. Mass spraying would then take place. By the time we returned in the evening, everything had been sanitised once again and fresh lotus blossoms had been placed on the pillows in our cool bungalows. Bats, birds and chameleons were spared the holocaust, although I can't think what they found to feed on.

It was a shock to see how very different the undeveloped Maldive island we visited was from our own comfortable one. The native people living there were tormented by flies, and their children all had running noses and coughs. The yards in front of their huts were dirty and unkempt; both the men and women looked unhappy and lethargic, half-heartedly trying to sell their little bits of jewellery or simply ignoring us. I felt an intruder in their lives.

This was one of the rare occasions on which the Italians I was with were quiet and subdued. Usually they were the noisiest group wherever we stayed. As the only English person among them, it was useless my trying to stay all reserved and proper. As far as the other groups staying on our island were concerned, I was Italian anyway, like the rest of my party.

It's an odd feeling to travel around a strange continent in the company of non-English people – a real identity crisis. I didn't know whether I was seeing this extraordinary Asian world through English or Italian eyes. At times I didn't know whether it was wiser to keep quiet about my nationality altogether. Our Sri Lankan guide in Colombo for example made no bones about his dislike of the British and the way they had exploited his country in the past. Shall I tell him I'm English, I wondered, or just keep quiet about it? Was I ashamed of the way we ruled? In a way I was, but it had all happened so long ago.

"I'm English, you know", I finally came out with as we walked through the Botanical Gardens in Kandy.

The guide showed neither surprise nor embarrassment.

"The English got what they could out of Sri Lanka" he said, "and they didn't care all that much about us."

We walked on and he pointed out a strange palm tree with clusters of large tropical fruits hanging like multiple testes from its crown of fonds.

No more was said about the British by either of us.

* * *

One thing is abundantly clear to me after so long in this country: the Italians are liked wherever they go in the world. Even the sorely-tried air hostesses on board the Luton-Palermo charters manage to smile at them at the end of their flight. They can't help it. Italians are never stand-offish; they're fun-loving and enthusiastic. I'm the stick-in-the-mud, the wet blanket, the law-abiding citizen who never raises her voice and always does her seat-belt up.

When I am on the platform at our local railway station and see the sign telling me that IT IS ABSOLUTELY FORBIDDEN TO CROSS THE LINE and even that UNDER NO CIRCUMSTANCES WHATSOEVER ARE PASSENGERS PERMITTED TO CROSS THE LINES, I don't cross. The Sicilians stream happily across regardless.

"Come on, Gay, what're you so worried about?"

"But it says you mustn't."

And what about that other notice at Palermo's Falcone and Borsellino airport warning that a 400.000 Lire fine will be given to anybody crossing the barrier in the arrival lounge? Four hundred thousand Lire! Why, that's £150. You wouldn't get me going near it. I just wait at a proper distance for my friends to appear off the plane.

The other night on television, the Minister for Health and two MPs were discussing the new anti-smoking bill which would prohibit smoking in more public places than come under the present ban. After quite a bit about tolerance and freedom of expression for hardened smokers, one of the MPs piped up and said nobody was likely to respect the law anyway.

"You know what we Italians are like," he began, "anything new which restricts our freedom is viewed with suspicion. Look at seat belts."

Now, where but in Italy would you expect the Minister of Health to smile and agree with that? Here he was quite openly taking it for granted that Italians would almost certainly ignore the proposed ban. In other words, he'd do his best, but what happened after that was not up to him.

"Gay, you're living in a completely different world" Franco tells me, "do you really, honestly believe it's any different in Britain today?"

Do I? And am I a happier person for my observance of the law? Am I a nicer person?

Of course not.

17
Of nuts, churches and markets

Autumn Sunday mornings are my favourite times for walking round the old parts of Palermo. What makes it so pleasing at this time is the blissful silence and the weather – mild, scented and golden which makes everything look beautiful. A friend of mine claims he has the most prestigious bathroom in the whole of Palermo because he can sit on the lavatory and look straight out over the orange cupolas of the twelfth-century church of St John of the Hermits, one of Sicily's loveliest buildings.

The guide books call St John's "suggestive" because *suggestivo* in Italian means delightful or enchanting. (A video on sale at the temple of Segesta I remember seeing recently also promises "the most suggestive sights of Sicily." The mind boggles.) Will I be translating like that in ten or so years time, I wonder.

The little church of St John of the Hermits is set in a garden at the top of a flight of stone steps which winds upwards through interlaced dense green leaves. Every plant and every tree is squashed up so close to its neighbour here that each has to fight for daylight. There's a giant monstera with leaves two feet across which has attached itself to the crumbling walls of the Benedictine cloisters and whose roots slither downwards to disappear into the cool waters of a stone tank below. Lemon, mandarin, grapefruit and pomegranate trees have all developed strangely tall or twisted trunks either through severe pruning or in order to reach the sun. The prickly pear plant is no longer a bush but a fully developed tree.

There are no keepers anywhere, the only trace of an official presence of any sort being the postcard man down at the entrance. He is immensely, unbelievably fat and sits precariously balanced on a low wall. His trousers are stretched over a vast belly and spread thighs, his eyes almost lost in the folds and flaps of great cheeks. He keeps up a running commentary on the marvels of the strips of coloured photographs he keeps beside him on the wall. Franco says the man has been sitting here in the same place for as long as he can remember, and that he hasn't changed at all. I feel that if he were to be accidentally dislodged from his wall, the postcard man would never rise again.

I wandered through the deep green aquarium world of the little garden as far as the convent walls. Children were practicing a sacred song somewhere deep inside and their achingly beautiful voices came floating through the iron grating at the windows.

When I left St John of the Hermits and started walking down towards the Royal Palace, I noticed a plain brown-painted door standing open a crack. As every building in this part of Palermo is extremely old and historic and likely to be in an advanced state of decay, the correct strategy is to try and get into anything you can, as you'll probably never get another chance. This place looked as if it might be a church. Dozens of them cluster around the mother cathedral here, some no more than simple chapels and all of them stuffed with an amazing collection of sculptures and paintings.

Inside, five men were talking together in the far corner of a large echoing chamber. At one time it certainly must have been a church; you could tell that straight away by the chubby sculptured marble cherubs holding up ornate swags all over the upper walls. Then there were the remains of two wooden choir stalls – very dusty and dark – some cream and gold-painted organ pipes high up under the roof and a pile of crimson moth-eaten brocade plonked at the top of the altar steps. The rest of the place was gutted. A handwritten notice on the wall said that this was the church of Sant Something and that a written history could be had on request.

It turned out the church had recently been cleaned out very thoroughly by burglars. The church warden – one of the men talking in the far corner – had apparently informed the police, and two officers had in due course come along to take an inventory of the stolen objects. These men – quite *scandalously* – had demanded the warden's and the priest's fingerprints.

"I told them, I said, what d'you want with our fingerprints? I asked. We

haven't stolen anything. I told Don Giuseppe (the priest) that the police wanted our fingerprints and he said we'd go along there. And when we went I said, what do you want with Don Giuseppe's and my fingerprints? I said I didn't see why we should leave our fingerprints."

All of this was delivered in rapid Sicilian to the attentive little audience who had gathered round him. Apart from myself this consisted of three men wearing patterned sweaters and anoraks with cameras and notebooks.

I wanted to know what the thieves had taken.

"Everything. There were two paintings, a Caravaggio..."

"A *Caravaggio*?"

"One was a Caravaggio, the other the school of Caravaggio, statues, goblets...." and so it went on.

I pointed to the printed notice and asked for the tourist leaflet on the church. The warden shook his head:

"No, no, haven't got it, don't know.. can't find..."

At the far end of the dark little passage running from the street door to the church proper, stood a bust of Jesus in a glass case. I thought it odd the thieves hadn't taken this with the rest of the stuff. Perhaps they'd found it just a little bit too lifelike. The bowed head was bleeding from the crown of thorns, the eyes downcast; the sort of thing that would have terrified a child.

No more than fifty paces further on was another almost identical church, this time intact and with the service just coming to an end. The same statuary, the same insets and sacred pictures, but pervaded here by the smell of incense and candles. Women in winter clothes in spite of the hot sunshine were streaming out onto the pavement and talking of lunch. I had to sidestep them.

Churches, churches and more churches. For Sicilian children they were an obligatory duty to be endured before you could think of enjoying yourself. Unless Franco showed written proof of attendance at the church of San Filippo Neri as a small boy, he would not be allowed into the gardens to play football. The gardens of course were church property – piously peopled with busts of saints and modestly shaded by huge subtropical trees. Although the saints are still there today, they now have to share their surroundings – rather disapprovingly I sometimes feel – with an open-air cinema.

Franco has never forgotten the beggars crowding round the entrance of the nearby San Francesco di Paola (the same church attended by Signora Durante, my enormous landlady) waiting for the congregation to come out. These were the years immediately after the war, when as many as thirty men would drag themselves forward on crutches or along the ground as soon as the people began to emerge from church. They had legs, arms or hands missing and some were horribly disfigured by burns.

These were war veterans who would never work again, the mentally deranged and the desperately poor. They're all gone now but there is still terrible poverty in Palermo. A missionary priest took me round one of the city's slum areas some years ago. It's behind my smart dentist's – a mass of alleyways and filthy squares that stretch down to the sea. I met families living in one-roomed hovels where there was one bed used by everybody, a lavatory pan and a stone sink covered by a piece of wood with a single gas ring on it.

* * *

Another church, this one massively columned and boarded up stands opposite the wonderful nut shop. Inside the nut shop, which isn't a proper shop at all, just a hole in the wall, stand brimming sacks of rice, barley, chickpeas, lentils, dried broad beans and meal, all with little steel shovels in them. Baskets and dishes of hazelnuts, almonds, peanuts, pistachios, lupin seeds and other strange things, cover all the other available space. It's so crowded in there that you can only get two people in at a time.

Two elderly unsmiling brothers stand behind the counter and shovel the nuts into cones which they make out of coarse grey paper. I bought a mixture of pumpkin seeds and chickpeas. Pumpkin seeds are wafer thin and have to be split lengthways between the two front teeth to get at the minute green kernel inside. If you're Sicilian the broken outer shell is spat noisily out onto the ground, if you're English it is discreetly eliminated into a closed fist. Chickpeas, as hard as ball bearings, have a pleasant musty flavour. They are tiny, round and bleached white, and three hundred grammes gets you several thousand. I'm addicted to them and to shelled hazelnuts. I also bought almonds for a cake, pistachios and roasted peanuts too because they're meant to be good for you.

Part of the pleasure of nuts of course is the speed at which you consume them – a good handful at a time straight from the paper cone. They're never so good once they're decanted into bowls.

* * *

I have to shout to the person beside me as we drive over the cobbles; with the car leaping and vibrating like this it's the only way you can make yourself heard. Bones rattle, teeth chatter, and the same bit of the dashboard of my Fiat Panda falls off in exactly the same place: right outside the Ucciardone prison walls.

Joined to this bleak and horrific 19th century building is the heavily protected bunker ("boonker") courtroom, custom-built for the Mafia trials of 1986. This is where I came to hear Tommaso Buscetta give evidence. The first of the *pentiti* or supergrasses, Buscetta changed people's idea of what the Mafia really was and how it was structured. He also made compulsive trial watching.

Part of the old Ucciardone prison looks out over smart apartment blocks and offices. You see prisoners' wives and mothers standing down in the road there shouting up to their husbands and sons inside the cells, and get glimpses of the men's faces at the barred windows. Sometimes the men wave their shirts on the ends of poles to show their women where they are. The armed guards controlling the ramparts take no notice.

The horror of life inside the Ucciardone prison can only be imagined. During Operation Clean Hands (which took off in 1992) when corruption suspects were being arrested every day in Italy, you realised how easily freedom could be curtailed. There is no bail granted to suspected persons in this country, so one can be flung into jail and left there for months (guilty or otherwise) without coming before the magistrates.

Corruption anyway it seems to me is an indefinable term in any kind of society. Many people must have received a gift at some time for their services. I don't mean fat sums of money in envelopes but far humbler offerings. Italy is still a rural-based society in many ways and in Sicily (and I imagine elsewhere on the mainland) gifts of cheeses, fruits, wine and so on are the norm for a favour or a special effort made for someone. Often it's simply helping the unwieldy bureaucratic machine to get moving. You may dislike (or like) the idea of being thanked in this way, but that's the way things are done. It's part of Italian life.

One Christmas, Franco came home and told me he had been given some *capretto*. This is the meat of the kid, very similar to lamb but even more delicious. To my great distress, when I went into the kitchen and opened the large canvas bag on the floor, there was a whole dead goat inside, hooves and all.

Over on the other side of the cobbled road, the overnight boat for Naples stands moored at the quay. It leaves every evening at 8.0, gliding gently into Naples harbour in the early hours of the following morning. I can never sleep in its claustrophobic cabins for the heat and thrumming of the engines, and would much prefer the posh Genoa-bound *Majestic* tied up there nearby which looks like a wonderful tiered wedding cake. The journey takes twice as long, but you get huge luxury cabins and smart restaurants.

The cobbles come to an end at last with one final lurch. I see in the mirror that the car behind me is getting far too close. The driver has hung a wooden crucifix complete with suffering Christ against his windscreen and propped a cheese grater up next to it.

Waiting at the fishmongers in the market to have my half kilo of fresh sardines slit open I heard the dirge-like music of a procession coming gradually closer. Sure enough a black-robed friar and two scarlet-cassocked choirboys soon appeared followed by a huge statue of the Madonna held aloft by men wearing dark purple jerkins over their shirts. Behind this came the components of a full brass band in braided jackets and peaked caps. The rear of the procession was brought up by a long trailing line of the faithful. Every few yards or so a hand bell would be rung and a voice would intone a prayer to the Madonna.

As the space between the market stalls was very narrow and crowded and the procession extremely bulky, I found myself forced back against the marble fish slab and the piles of discarded cabbage leaves round my ankles. There was no question at all of trying to hurry on ahead of the robed friar – it just wouldn't have done. You simply waited respectfully until the whole train had passed by. I was only a foot or so away from one of the little choirboys picking his nose and yawning. Behind him, the men shouldering the heavy wooden poles under the statue were streaming with sweat.

The calendar of feastday processions is a very ancient one in Palermo with the most magnificent of all being that of the patron saint Santa Rosalia. I have never got used to seeing the mayor of the city in his green, white and red chest ribbon walking solemnly next to the Cardinal at the head of this procession. It seems so odd for cultured, urbane men to pay public homage to a mythical miracle worker. Rather as if John Major were to speak at a remembrance service for Robin Hood. But then I haven't got a Catholic background, nor have I grown up in a Mediterranean culture. Of course the presence of the civil authorities is no more than a gesture on their part, yet I still find it incompatible with modern life.

"Don't you agree that Palermo is the most European of the Italian cities?" a woman once asked me shoving a microphone under my mouth.

"No", I said, "quite the contrary." For in many ways it couldn't be more un-European.

The defending counsel in a recent court case claimed this part of the deep south of Italy to be very different indeed. The case involved a murder committed on Pantelleria, an island off the southwest coast of Sicily. A man had been found brutally battered to death in his wrecked car at the bottom of a cliff. The body had lain there undetected for several days and would probably have remained for even longer had not someone noticed a bird flying down to the same spot day after day. The gruesome story was that the bird had found a good source of food in the decomposing body.

In his final summing up the counsel for the defence pointed out that Pantelleria was nearer to the African continent than to Europe and that the three accused were therefore victims of (in his opinion) an almost primitive society.

I have no experience of life on Pantelleria; it's a very popular tourist resort in summer and, I imagine, a desperately lonely place for the remainder of the year.

18
Public and private

Wanda Osiris, the famous soubrette, died some weeks ago aged eighty-nine. That wasn't her real name of course; she was probably christened the Italian equivalent of Edna May Jenkins or something. Anyway, her forte was coming down a curved and brilliantly-lit stairway with an armful of roses, singing:

"*Ti parlerò-o d'amo-o-r!*" ("I'll speak to you of lo-ove!") in an atrociously off-key soprano voice.

The staircase was always bordered by her "boys" all down on one knee with arms outstretched, and all gazing adoringly up at her. She was very blond and very gorgeously dressed, yet could neither dance nor sing. She was no beauty either, but apparently had great charm and stage presence.

Wanda Osiris was way before I came to Italy, yet I did see her once or twice on television in guest appearances. Swathed in white fox fur and fake diamonds, she would reminisce on the old days to roars of applause from a youthful studio audience who weren't even thought of, let alone born, when she was performing.

"Oh, those stage-door johnnies, darling! And the gifts we were given! I had invitations from the richest men in the world; we used to go out on their yachts and eat off silver dishes...ah, you young ones now have no idea how we were fêted then!"

I don't know whether Wanda ever appeared in Palermo; if she did, it would probably have been at the Politeama theatre. Looking as though it might have been built for circuses, this massive construction has an apron stage and was used for reviews and musical comedy. I imagine the red-plush stalls date back to that period and might have replaced the original sawdust ring. There are still the circular ringside seats as well as two tiers of boxes, and hard, narrow benches set steeply round the theatre and stretching right up into the dome. I doubt whether you would have seen anything at all from those top seats or indeed whether it was possible to fill such a huge place at all.

The theatre is fashioned on a Roman coliseum with great echoing arches built on different storeys behind the auditorium, and narrow passageways (just the right size for lions?) running in towards the centre. You get a vivid picture of chariots careering round and round the ring, sparks flying from their wheels, especially when you glance up at those Pompeii-like Roman figures round the walls. But the dimly-lit and silent passageways on these upper storeys are also ghostly and I always get a nightmarish sensation of never being able to find my way out again.

Wanda and her entourage may have entered through one of the massive outside arches marked CAVALLI (HORSES) down in the street. I don't think she would have liked that very much. Palermo boys who wanted to see the show without buying a ticket used to sneak in through the CAVALLI entrance. Franco once got caught doing it. After managing to get in he had clambered right up beyond the top row of the gods to escape detection, only to find a fireman installed up there in the roof.

"Here you, what the hell do you think you're doing up here? Go on, get out!"

Bit different from my first review which my grandmother took me to see in the West End.

You mean you never thought of slipping in free?

Deary – me, no, whatever next? Why, it never entered our heads to cheat; we were *English*.

The show was fantastic and very grown-up; lovely plush seats and a box of dark chocolates in the interval. I remember my grandmother saying bits of it were vulgar but I didn't notice anything.

Other activities for older boys in Palermo in the fifties were the visits to one of the city's brothels. These legalised houses functioned in Italy right up until 1958 when they were closed down by what is known as the Merlin law. Nothing to do with the wizard, just the name of the Socialist (woman) politician who proposed and got the law passed. There was a brothel called Yolanda's just off the Via Roma, another more up-market known as Le Rose, nearby. I was terribly curious about the set-up, about what actually went on in there. Did you have to pay before or after, and what were the women like?

From what I could gather, the men went into a pleasant, largish drawing room where the girls were, waiting perhaps in a wrap or their underclothes – slip and stockings and so on – and more or less chose the one they wanted. The financial transaction took place at a desk where the client would be given a small metal token which he would later consign to the girl in her bedroom. There would then be a bit of small talk between client and girl so as not to make the object of the visit too obvious, and after that both went off. Services rendered were varied but didn't I think, stretch to anything too exotic or kinky.

These brothels or "closed houses" as they were known, were as respectable as such places could be; sleaze had nothing to do with the set-up at all – indeed, there might well have been a crucifix or a picture of the Madonna on the bedroom wall. Hygiene too, was scrupulously observed with the girls being regularly examined by a doctor for signs of venereal disease. Yet in spite of this attention to their welfare (which after all was simply keeping the goods in prime condition), the women were employees in a business concern like any other, and as such, subject to taxes like everybody else. Unlike other categories though, they appeared in police records, which meant they were branded for life.

Angelina Merlin saw something very wrong in this – in the state making money from prostitution. She presented a bill to have the houses shut down for good. Opinion was divided on the wisdom of this move, and clients were invited to sign petitions for or against. Many of the younger girls who worked in the brothels, mostly those in their early twenties, were in favour. They believed – rightly so – that once legalised prostitution was abolished, their police records would cease to exist as a result, and this would leave them free to begin a new life.

In some cases this did in fact happen; one girl who used to work in the Palermo brothels went to the Apuglia region in the south where she opened a dry cleaners. She later married. But again, all this was long before I came to Sicily. By the time I arrived, the young Sicilians we met had either never known brothels or if they had, (naturally enough) saw no reason to talk about them. But I found their history interesting.

The Catholic Church's condemnation of any form of carnal knowledge before marriage had been enough to nip most relationships in their sexual bud. Girls – and not only in Sicily – were so strictly supervised by their families that boys were forced to frequent prostitutes. Ironically – at least to anyone brought up in a non-Catholic country like England – the brothels were seen by Italian families as serving a real need: an initiation into manhood as it were. (No such relief was contemplated for daughters.) So the "closed houses" served a physiological need, as was obvious from the youthful age of their clientele. With the abolition of the brothels, two things happened: one was that prostitutes now appeared on the streets, and secondly, the strict control of girls began to be very slightly relaxed.

That was the situation some years before I arrived. If I'd known a bit more about Italian social history perhaps I wouldn't have been so amazed by the attention foreign girls received in Sicily. Scandinavians and Germans were the most sought-after; it didn't matter if they were Valkyrie seconds with legs like tree trunks, their blond hair was enough to make the Sicilians come flocking. The English were OK but not considered of the first order, the women traditionally thought of as being flat-chested bespectacled females with hang-ups on sex.

Oh dear.

But then, hadn't the English always considered Italians over-sexed and as for the Sicilians..... well we know how hot-bloodied *they* are, dear, don't we?

They are. A Palermo friend told me that when he goes to donate blood, it comes out bubbling and steaming into the syringe. I believe him.

* * *

Doctor Coletti held his surgery in the gatehouse of a baroque palazzo in Palermo. You had to push past overgrown oleander bushes to get to the door. Inside was the spartan waiting room with three or four antique chairs and, leading off this, the surgery proper. Both rooms had tiled floors and were damp and cold. There were only two tiny windows so it was also very dim.

Doctor Coletti had a thick grey-white moustache and looked rather like Albert Schweitzer. I suppose he must have been in his seventies when I first knew him. He sat behind a desk piled high with samples of medicines left him by a succession of drug company reps, and the surgery was always in a fug from his chain-smoking. Perhaps this was why the desk lamp was always left on. He coughed a lot as a result of the smoking and smelt very strongly of wine; I'm sure it was terribly unhealthy in there.

I don't mean to caricature Doctor Coletti; he was an exceptionally good person and an unhappy one. I think his wife had left him for another man, and that was when he started to drink. He was always caring and patient and had a joking way of minimising any anxieties one had. I once went to him feeling awful and not knowing what on earth was wrong with me. He diagnosed me at once as having food poisoning. I don't know whether he was right or not – I don't even know if he was a good doctor – but I began to feel better almost at once.

I never found out why he used the gatehouse as a surgery. It is still there, tucked away just as I remember it near the imposingly carved gateway of the big house. In spite of being dreadfully run-down like all the others in this part of Palermo, the villa is still defiantly upright in the midst of its vast unkempt grounds. The owners have converted part of these into a garden centre to help with its upkeep, and they also hire out a suite of high-ceilinged ballrooms for wedding receptions. But like so many Sicilians, they just don't seem to be able to get to grips with their bricks and mortar heritage, and one wonders how much longer the house can fight off total decay.

A friend of mine lives in another huge pile not far from here. The entire area, known as The Plain of Hills (whatever a plain of hills is) was where the monied and the titled liked to build their country retreats between the seventeenth and eighteenth centuries. It takes me a good twenty minutes to walk past her estate which is mostly planted out with cabbages and lemon trees.

Both these villas have somehow managed to survive as family homes – others have given up the ghost and been acquired by the town council. I used to take my children to one of these – a rather superior old villa in another part of town surrounded by a magical overgrown jungle peopled by headless statues and empty fountain basins. It was never made clear whether one was allowed into the garden or not; a rusty sign stuck into the earth at the entrance proclaimed:

Access to the public has been suspended

which was ambiguous enough. But, I thought, to say access was *suspended* surely implied that at some distant point in Palermo's history it had been granted, so I always walked in.

Occasionally I was stopped by the caretaker who shot out of his gatehouse under the banyan tree like a conger eel and said I couldn't go in.

"But I came yesterday" I told him "and last week, and nobody said anything."

"Well, it's not allowed." He jerked his head towards the rusty sign.

"Oh dear" I sighed, "then we'll just have to go home again. I'm sorry children, the man says he won't let us in."

Moved, the caretaker relented: "Well then, just for this once. But it's not allowed, you know. I'm letting you in as a special favour."

One way of avoiding this comedy act was to walk through the entrance very quickly and purposefully – if possible carrying a briefcase. You are never stopped anywhere in Sicily when you walk quickly and purposefully. Conversely, failure is always guaranteed by creeping enquiringly forward and asking permission. There is something in the congenital make-up of caretakers, doormen, and ushers which makes them refuse any request right out. It doesn't matter whether you have an appointment to see a doctor in out-patients at the hospital or have to see someone in an office, you are still made to feel you have absolutely no right to be there. They take a positive glee in putting obstacles in your path.

In yet another of Palermo's public gardens where you have to squirm sideways through a crack left open between the heavily padlocked gates, the keeper eyes me suspiciously:

"Yes?"

This time the notice on the gate actually tells me the hours it is open to the public: nine a.m.– sundown. And by now I have been living in Palermo for a good many years.

"Yes *what*?"

"What did you want?"

"I'm going into the garden. What d'you think I want?"

"Ah."

And in I sweep.

All this is almost as infuriating as coming up against the tollgate-keeper at Mondello. He presides over one of my favourite walks which goes from this local seaside town for about a mile along the cliffs to the tip of the promontory. You have the sea all the way along on your right and soaring mountains on your left. It's blissfully quiet after the roar of Palermo.

For some unknown reason, this stretch of coastline is private property. Or so it would seem. In fact, you have to pay a toll at the gate. However you only have to pay the toll if you go in by car; if you walk, it's free. In warm weather the keeper can be found slumped in a deckchair by the roadside watching an old television set placed on top of an empty crate. The last time I went, he was sitting rapt before a commercial:

"Ah, I've caught you using my deodorant again, Carlo," a girl was saying playfully to her boyfriend, give it here!"

"How come you have all the best things? No, I'm going to keep it for myself. It's my deodorant now."

Close-up of the man's shaved armpit being dampened by a fine spray. Smooth little bubbles materialise from the nozzle and melt gently into his skin.

Voice over: "no harmful ingredients, only cool, soothing lanoline."

"Carlo!"

The girl was swung, laughing delightedly, into the man's arms, her glossy hair brushing his face.

At that point a car could be heard approaching; it stopped by the gate. The keeper eased himself out of the deckchair and swaggered over to the car window.

"Ten thousand lire."

He hardly glanced at me at all as I walked past.

It's all to do with territorial rights and the lack of clearly-marked barriers. A park may be public property but the keeper is employed to keep watch there, so in part it's his too. You see it all over Sicily. Take the case of the tennis for instance.

The court where I occasionally play belongs to a smart housing estate. Set inside the estate's communal gardens, it backs directly onto an old house outside, so is enclosed on three sides by wire netting and on the fourth by the house wall.

You'd think it would be rather a nuisance for the people living there when the ball comes crashing against their outside wall, especially as the court is nothing to do with them, but they don't seem to mind. The signora pegs out her washing quite happily on the flat roof, and her husband often wanders out peaceably in his vest to watch our game. Perhaps they feel – very reasonably so – that being materially part of a someone else's property gives them certain rights over it. Besides, they're animal lovers and like feeding the stray cats.

Every time I play up their end of the court I have to be careful not to trip over these cats who go backwards and forwards across the court on their way to feed. The soggy mass of cooked pasta with tomato sauce the signora provides them with is let slowly and carefully down on a rope in a plastic bag to land just behind the base line. A particularly hard shot from my opponent can land dangerously near the plastic bag – and very occasionally hit it full force. Last week, seeing the cats streaking across to their bulging meal, the signora leant over:

"They've got meat in it today" she called down to me proudly.

"How nice" I called back.

I felt I should be apologising for playing there in the first place and getting in the cats' way, so in charge did she seem. What I secretly hoped for of course, was that a ball would get them hard in the ribs and send them leaping from the court.

Cats apart, some places are quite definitely private and as such, have to be protected. Palermo banks for instance take elaborate precautions against armed robberies. The more sophisticated and ingenious these become, the more stressful life gets for clients. My local bank uses the reinforced glass cubicle with the electronically-controlled doors.

Although it is part of one of Italy's largest banking concerns, the tiny branch in my *borgata* is extremely laid-back as far as efficiency goes. The uniformed security guard in the too-tight navy blue trousers strolling up and down outside will do his best to help if you get trapped inside the cubicle. Clients are meant to leave any metal objects in the lock-up pigeon holes in the entrance before entering the bank, and a recorded voice will remind them to do so. Although the staff often forget to activate this voice, I always comply, just in case.

Last time, after locking away my handbag, I discovered that the key to my pigeon hole had no number on it. I pointed this out to the bank clerk inside.

"Good heavens, yes!" she laughed delightedly "I hope you remember which is your number!"

"Don't you think you should get new tags put on them, though?" I asked her.

"Mm, we certainly should. Now, what can I do for you?"

To get into the bank in the first place I have to press a red button to make the outer door swing towards me. If this works correctly I go through, and the door closes behind me. I am now inside the minute cubicle. After what should be a split second, the inner door wheezes open and I find myself inside the bank.

It would be untrue to say this system always works; more frequently than not, both glass doors swing open and shut at the same time, so you have to make a dash for it. Alternatively, you get trapped in the cubicle while both doors sigh open an inch and sigh shut again. This is when the security guard outside will lend assistance.

"Wait!" he commands the distraught face behind the glass, holding up the flat of his hand.

"Come out!"

"I don't seem to be able to........"

"Come out. NOW!"

I had to renew some bonds and wanted to speak to the clerk I usually deal with. I asked the cashier where she was.

"She's just popped out to the post office" he told me "she'll only be about half and hour."

Half an hour? Could he see to it for me?

"Ooh no, sorry Signora. No, no, I can't do that for you; dear me no. You'll have to wait."

Another recorded voice – this time a woman's – addresses you as you prepare to leave the bank:

"*Arriverderci*" she purrs sexily, "and please don't forget to collect your belongings from the pigeon hole."

The bemused man in the *coppola* inside the cubicle, was answering her:

"No I won't , thank you," he said," goodbye."

* * *

Palermo's streets and squares are undeniably public property – litter-strewn like a lot of other large cities, yet freer of the sad bundles of humanity you see on Rome's or London's pavements. Of course you do come across the homeless and the mad wandering about or slumped on church steps; yesterday on the crowded 101 bus for instance, I sat in front of a burly, unshaven man wearing the permanent wide-eyed smile of the simple-minded. Every few minutes he would call out in broad Sicilian to the ticket inspector at the back,

"You can see my ticket, I've got it! I've got it!"

I suppose someone had warned him of the current crack-down on public transport fare-dodging. He was breathing heavily and shifting about on his seat behind me and I was half expecting it when he tapped on my shoulder. I turned round. He thrust his ticket under my nose;

"Look, look."

"That's very good" I told him, "you've bought your ticket. Quite right."

I got off before him at the Politeama Square. This was where a couple of years ago a group of schoolchildren had traced the outlines of dead bodies all over the paving stones. Half of them had lain down and flung out their limbs in attitudes of violent death while the others had painted round them. The purpose was to remind people of all those who had been murdered by the Mafia.

The local paper had announced the demonstration by saying the students would be chalking in the outlines, but in point of fact, here they were using pots of very permanent-looking red, blue yellow and green paint. The question I couldn't answer was whether it was right to cover a public square in paint which wouldn't disappear until the next rains in four months time, or until (in the unlikely event), they were removed by the authorities; or whether on the contrary, it was right that an indelible trace should remain.

"At least nobody will forget this way" a teacher said when I voiced my doubt," like they've forgotten all the people murdered by the Mafia in this island. I hope with all my heart the drawings never do get rubbed out!"

They're still faintly visible today.

Enzo Biagi, one of Italy's best-known and successful journalists recently interviewed one of the killers of Judge Giovanni Falcone, a *pentito* helping, as they say, the police with their enquiries.

"What do you regret?" Biagi asked him, after listening to the man's life story and the cold-blooded way the murder had been planned and executed,

There was a very brief pause.

"That I was born in Sicily" came the reply.

I found this particularly shocking and tragic. It threw a completely new light on the Sicilians' attitude towards their own land. Public gardens, tennis courts, and everything else.

19

Solunto

I dialled the number of the offices of the tourist magazine I write for.
"Hello?"
Could I speak to the editor?
"Erm, I'm not sure if she's free at the moment. Hang on a moment, will you?"
There was a second's silence before Beethoven's *Fur Elise* came down the phone played far too quickly on the piano.
The furious pace of the music annoyed me even more than having to wait to speak to the editor. *Fur Elise* may well be considered a simple piece given to beginners to play, but it should be executed *poco moto*, not prestissimo like this.In fact the pianist was getting through it so fast that we were round at the beginning again before I had time to shift the receiver to the other ear.
I dislike recorded music on the phone because it allows people to be rude to you in a polite way. You may have to hang on for five minutes or more Signora, but at least you've been provided with music. Maybe *Fur Elise* hadn't been properly regulated by the secretary at the offices; perhaps there was a knob on the tape recorder which had been turned too far to the right. After I had heard six complete renderings, I was put through to the editor.
I was going to do a piece on Solunto for the magazine and wanted to know how much space she could let me have. Solunto is an ancient city – either Roman or Greek I can never remember which – about sixteen kilome-

tres from Palermo. If I am feeling depressed or if I sometimes wish I had never left England, Solunto will make everything all right. It's in the most beautiful setting, splayed over the top of a mountain overlooking a great green plain. Beyond is the sea and the curved protecting arm of the little harbour of Porticello. Although it is a complete city like Pompeii with streets, market place, public baths and so on, it has fewer buildings still upright. The cobbled roads crossing each other at right angles are still solidly underfoot, so are the occasional glimpses of blue and ochre mosaic floor, but I think what makes Solunto such a magical, mystical place is not so much its ruins as the quiet beauty of its hillsides. Or maybe it's a perfect combination of the two.

Here, arthritic little olive trees bend carefully over to examine the dusty dry soil which teems with crickets and fragments of broken pottery. I like to walk beneath the trees, following one of the old streets that lead away from the city through the long scratchy grasses to the edge of the hillside. The roads must once have led somewhere, but now just come to an end between great lichened boulders and stiff, dried poppy heads. There's a warm pungent scent of rosemary and geranium leaves up here and everything's a very long way off – the church bells down in the plain, the larksong above, the sea.

The wall and floor decorations in Solunto – the stucco cornices and lozenge patterns, or "lively frescoes" as the guide book calls them, aren't a patch on the beauty of their natural surroundings. A painting of Leda and the Swan, considered the *pièce de résistance* of the ruins, is to be found on the triclinium on the north-west side of the peristylium in one of the houses. I have no recollection whatsoever of Leda or for that matter of tricliniums or peristyliums although I must have seen them. I also learn from the guide book that you "may ask one of the guardians to open the gate to this room" and I certainly never remember doing *that*.

Behold a sudden vision of myself in thick tweeds and brogues, striding along the Agora past the elliptic cisterns and the tabernae and rapping on the door of the cubiculum with my shooting stick:

"My good man, be so kind as to unlock the gate to this house immediately so that I may see Leda on the triclinium."

It's a pity I never did get in there, as the same room apparently contains "a naked male figure seated between winged female figures carrying torches" which I should very much like to have perused.

I learned in the course of my research (or was reminded again) that Solunto goes back to the fourth century BC, and that it was one of three Punic cities in Sicily founded before the Greek colonisation of the island. It came under Carthaginian and Roman rule before mysteriously disappearing without trace in the Middle Ages. Excavations on it only began in 1825, and apparently there is still a great deal more to be brought to light. A far older settlement which was razed to the ground by Dionysius of Syracuse and which archeologists think lies fairly close by, has never been uncovered.

Italy of course has a glut of these old cities; one of my favourites, after Solunto, is Ostia Antica just outside Rome. When I was in the capital not long ago with a morning to spare, I decided to go along there.

Ostia is like Solunto in that the natives never bother to visit it. Unlike the Sicilian city though, it is at sea level and spread over an enormous area which takes all day to cover. It is also severely cultural with only a museum and postcard shop and nowhere at all to have a drink or a sandwich.

"Now for heaven's sake, take a picnic lunch with you" my friends told me, "there's absolutely nothing there, and you'll be dying for a drink."

I didn't, because my idea was to do Ostia for a couple of hours and then have a snack afterwards in the town. And I did walk round for two hours among the red brick buildings and the umbrella pines, but that of course brought me deep into the heart of the ancient city without any hope of reaching the exit for at least a couple more hours. The sun was climbing towards its midday zenith and it was swelteringly hot. "I'm not thirsty" I told myself, "what magnificent ruins." And kept going.

Ostia is so vast that even if there are hundreds of tourists wandering about there, you are quite likely never to come across any of them. Not only are there interminable roads lined by many-roomed houses to explore, there are also apartment blocks, warehouses, multi-storey theatres, market places and an entire mosaic-lined mall. And so it goes on.

Just as I was about to flag out completely, I came to a wonderful pine wood; it was shady and cool and had smooth, flat stones where weary bones could rest. There wasn't a soul about. I found a perfect place on the cool soft ground between two of these flat stones, lay down on my back and closed my eyes.

After barely five minutes, I heard a woman's voice, then another, then a man's. Suddenly, the wood was full of bellowing, laughing people. I sat up appalled. It was obviously an organised group who, as I could tell from their accents, came from the Emilia Romagna region in the north.

Worse was to come: one of the women came right over to my stone and called out:

"Here, over here! I've found the perfect spot!"

And the whole contingent – twenty of thirty of them – closed in on me. I couldn't believe it. Not one of them thought that they might possibly be intruding on my privacy. No that isn't true; as they sat down comfortably and full of jollity in front, behind and next to me and began opening their packed lunches, one woman looked up with a rueful smile:

"I'm afraid we've ruined your peaceful nap!"

I stood up – I had to – and moved further off to a far less smooth stone where I couldn't possibly lie down. All around, the party from Emilia Romagna were unwrapping their delicious sandwiches and pulling out bottles of cool mineral water. A large robust matron munching greedily looked over at me surprised and said

"Aren't you eating too?"

I shook my head, quite sure now I was going to be offered a roll and a cup of water. Italians are always so generous with their food. But not a bit of it. She looked away again and went on stuffing.

When they were all replete, they lay back on the ground and took a nap. I shall never forget it.

* * *

Back at Solunto, I took a look round the pleasant little museum. My little guide book tells me that "attention should be drawn on two female statues in room 1." Tut tut, I really must have a word with the compilers; we really can't have that sort of thing, can we? Attention should be drawn *to*, not *on*..... I also learn that "only the lower part of the marble statue of a magistrate is still extant." What has happened to the top half I wonder. Probably inextant.

Still, mustn't carp; I've made some howlers myself.

Below, through the museum windows, I can see a train slowly crossing the plain on its way to Messina. They're starting to build up a metropolitan railway network in Palermo now; not entirely underground because much of it uses the existing overland track, but quite a bit of it does run through tunnels.

Used to the trusty old 1960s Bakerloo line (West Hampstead to Charing Cross and back), I found Palermo's tube a bit feeble. There are still only about five stations, none of them are remotely near where you want to go. Still, I thought I'd try it one morning just to see what it was like.

As the train drew into our local station and stopped I saw the driver get out onto the platform and start walking towards us. It turned out he had recognised Franco. The two of them began chatting.

"Come up and ride in the engine with me " he said to us.

This seemed a bit irregular to me. But in we went.

"Go on," he said to me as we thundered through one of the tunnels, "take the controls."

"Good God no" I said shocked, "I couldn't."

"Go on, there's nothing to it."

That was how I came to be driving a train on the Palermo underground. Only for a minute or two of course.

The sun was about to go down over Solunto. I still felt contented and pleased with the world. Not a hint of nostalgia for England, no sudden remembered jab of anger or frustration to remind me of the trials of Sicilian life. Just peace and universal love. Nothing is ever as bad as it seems – not if there are places like this. The shadows lengthened and the keeper told us it was time to go.

A phone call

About ten days after the dinner party for Harold Acton, I had a call from Dr Johnson.

"I've read your book" he said.

I waited.

"There is much I liked in it" the voice came again "but I am not sure you have understood what I said about humility."

"Humility" I said, "in what sense?"

"In the sense that it is always intended my dear lady: the ability to humble ourselves before others, to be aware of our own failings and not to laud what we believe to be superior qualities over those we deem of little importance in our fellow men."

"I hope I haven't given that impression, it is not what I feel at all."

"That's as may be" he said. "I am also at a loss to understand why you should wish to give your book such a title: *Harold Acton Was My Hero*..... I am sure Mr Acton is a very worthy man – indeed I have seen so for myself – yet I cannot help but feel that your experience has been far richer and more varied than his..."

"Yes, but you see, I wanted to....."

"On another score, I am particularly struck by your descriptions of Mediterranean funeral rites and the cult of miracles in Sicily, something with which I had no immediate experience.I should be greatly indebted – when you have sufficient time at your disposal – if you would furnish me with more details of Sicilian manifestations. You may use this very means of communication we are engaged in at this moment. The telephone really is a most excellent invention."

"Dr Johnson..." I began.

"To return to the matter in hand: one should never smile upon the religious beliefs of others you know, neither should the particular characteristics or (as we may see them) foibles, of foreign peoples be always taken in a lighthearted vein.."

Oh dear, has the man no sense of humour?

"The women of easy virtue you mention in the Favorita park, the poor villagers in their widows' weeds – and even the delinquents – are all victims of an unjust and greedy society; this we should never forget. However, I was greatly diverted Madam, by your experiences of teaching the English language in Palermo. I hope you will permit me to send you a signed copy of my Dictionary to assist you in your difficulties over grammar."

"That's very kind of you Dr Johnson, but I wouldn't risk the Italian postal system if I were you, I don't think it would ever get here."

"No? That surprises me greatly; then I must wait until you return to these shores. Our language you know, is our great heritage and should be preserved for posterity. By the by, I spoke to her Majesty the other day; she has not yet had time to read your book but assures me she intends to do so during the Christmas recess. I have heard nothing on the other hand, from Mr James Joyce, but then did not expect to. The Irish are a most peculiar and hysterical race who would benefit greatly from being civilised."

So much for tolerance and humility, I thought.

"You have already and most kindly quoted me at the beginning of your book" Johnson went on, "allow me now to make recourse to the admirable Juvenal and furnish you with a fitting epilogue."

And in a slow and sonorous voice that came down the telephone wire punctuated by heavy, asthmatic breathing, he began to intone:

"Quidquid agunt homines, votum timor ira voluptas
  Gaudia discursus nostri farrago libelli est"

"I gave up Latin when I was fifteen, Dr Johnson" I said, "you'll have to translate for me."

There was a brief impatient snort from the other end.

"All that men are engaged in, their wishes, fears, anger, pleasures, joys, and varied pursuits, form the hotch-potch of my book."

"Yes that's true," I replied, *"I like that. E poi, pensandoci bene, non ci sono delle vere differenze fra noi, non è vero? In fondo – italiani, inglesi – siamo tutti uguali."*

"What? What's that you said?"

"I said: 'And what's more, thinking it over, there aren't any real differences between us, are there? Italians or English – underneath, we're all the same.'"

END